Travels with
Elvis

OTHER BOOKS ABOUT ELVIS PRESLEY
FROM RANDOM HOUSE VALUE PUBLISHING, INC.:

FIT FOR A KING

ARE YOU HUNGRY TONIGHT?

ELVIS: THE KING OF ROCK 'N' ROLL

Travels with
Elvis

A GUIDE ACROSS AMERICA TO ALL THE PLACES
WHERE THE KING LIVED, LOVED, AND LAUGHED

JACK BARTH

GRAMERCY BOOKS
NEW YORK

This 1999 edition is published by Gramercy Books™, an imprint of Random House Value Publishing, Inc., 201 East 50th Street, New York, NY 10022, by arrangement with NTC/Contemporary Publishing Company.

Gramercy Books™ and design are trademarks of Random House Value Publishing, Inc.

Printed in the United States of America

(Previously published as: *Roadside Elvis*)

Random House
New York • Toronto • London • Sydney • Auckland
http://www.randomhouse.com/

Library of Congress Cataloging-in-Publication Data
Barth, Jack.
    [Roadside Elvis]
    Travels with Elvis: a guide across America to all the places
where the King lived, loved, and laughed / Jack Barth.
        p.   cm.
    Originally published as: Roadside Elvis: the complete state-by-
state travel guide for Elvis Presley fans. Chicago: Contemporary
books, c1991.
    Includes bibliographical references (p. ***) and index.
    ISBN 0-517-20309-X
    1. Presley, Elvis, 1935-1977—Homes and haunts—Guidebooks.
2. Presley, Elvis, 1935-1977—Miscellanea.   I. Title.
ML420.P96B43   1999
782.42166'092—dc21   98-35933
                                                              CIP
                                                              MN

8 7 6 5 4 3 2 1

Contents

Hey, Thanks

I'd like to figuratively drape a silklike Vegas scarf around the shoulders of my TCB crew: Michael Carlisle and Elizabeth Ziemska. Todd Morgan of Graceland is a fine fellow who provided reliable info—even though he wouldn't let me work at Graceland like I wanted. Bill E. Burk punctured a lot of myths and steered me right, especially in the Memphis chapter. (I highly recommend his quarterly magazine *ELVIS WORLD*—to subscribe, write Bill at Box 16792, Memphis, TN 38186-0792.) Jay Orr at the *Nashville Banner* filled in some blanks there. Several fan clubbers helped and since they were so responsive to me, I bet they'll be responsive to you if you join their clubs (see Elvis Fan Clubs). A big thanks goes to them, too.

Introduction
Next Exit, Elvis

The book you are about to read is the result of an exhaustive search for places all across the country that are of interest to Elvis fans. No stone—literal or metaphorical—has been left unturned in uncovering the gamut of Elvisness that can be found all over your, my, and Elvis's favorite land.

Travels with Elvis takes you to the places and people that Elvis touched. What you'll also find are relics of people who were important to him or to his musical roots; these are the forces that came together to form the King of Rock & Roll.

What you won't find are any reports of "Elvis sightings." These are totally stupid fabrications that have been pumped up by the totally stupid media. Elvis's spirit will forever live in the hearts and minds of those who love him, but in the physical sense Elvis is dead, dead, dead. If he were still alive, do you think he'd be taking a chance on Lisa Marie giving away Graceland to the Scientologists? (Besides, everybody knows that it's his twin brother, Jesse, not Elvis, who's still alive.)

One note of caution when using this book: call ahead if you plan a long trip to an Elvis mecca. These things come and go faster than you can say "Stop, look, and listen, baby, that's my philosophy/It's called rubberneckin', baby, but that's all right with me." Prices and hours will change, too. Especially prices.

There are a lot more ways to explore Elvis's life than by visiting Graceland every August 16. For the true Elvis fan, this is the only travel guide worth its weight in road-trip fun.

Jack Barth

1
U.S.A.

We begin not in 1935 Tupelo, where Elvis himelf began, but in the U.S.A. today, where Elvis reigns more regally than ever. Elvis toured incessantly in the 1950s and 1970s, trekking to every corner of America. But it's not only his bootprints we are seeking. There are beckoning gift shops, heartfelt tributes, exciting movie locations, glamorous Elvis imitators, and hotel rooms where the King slept. (In fact, at some of the less renovated hotels, you just might get to sleep in the very same bed in which Elvis himself copped his royal Zs!—though if you want to emulate his vampire hours you'd better request a late checkout.)

...And, as always, much, much more!!!!

ALABAMA

Alabama was the childhood home of the man who discovered Elvis, the man who "doctored" Elvis, and the Elvis of country music.

Anniston: Dr. Nick (George C. Nichopoulos) began treating Elvis for saddle sores in 1967, soon after Elvis acquired his Mississippi ranch. He became Elvis's personal physician, ultimately being labeled by hard-hitting investigative telejournalist Geraldo Rivera as "The Man Who Killed Elvis." In late 1990, Dr. Nick tried to grab some media attention by claiming that Elvis was murdered.

Dr. Nick grew up here in a white frame house. His dad, Constantine, better known as Gus, ran a restaurant. George attended Woodstock Grammar School, now the **Woodstock Professional Building**, at 409 East 10th Street. In his teen years he went to Anniston High School, where he played football and became an Eagle Scout. The building was torn down in 1972.

Gus is buried in **Highland Cemetery**, at East 10th Street and Highland Avenue. Dr. Nick, who was shot at by a sniper at a football game after the Rivera accusations, still practices in Memphis (see Memphis).

Clanton: In 1954, R. W. Blackwood and Bill Lyles of the Blackwood Brothers gospel quartet were killed near town in a plane crash after a show. Young Elvis grieved when he heard the news. When his buddy Cecil Blackwood, a member of the Songfellows, moved into the Blackwood group to fill the void, Elvis auditioned for his job, but the future King was turned down.

Decatur: Decatur was the hometown of blues singer Charlie Burse, who was born in 1901 and died in 1965. One story goes that Elvis saw him wigglin' in a concert on Beale Street and got some ideas about motorizing his own torso.

Sam Phillips worked as a disc jockey at Decatur's WHSL in 1943. WHSL is still on the airwaves today. Another station of interest is WHOS, which went from gospel to an all-Elvis format in mid-1988, but unfortunately dropped it about six months later. A spokesperson says the Elvis format generated a lot of media interest, but not much listenership. WHOS is now a country station and has no future Elvis plans.

Florence: Florence was the birthplace of two musical heavyweights, blues pioneer W.C. Handy, who was born in 1873, and Sam Phillips, who was born in 1923. Phillips was the son of a tenant farmer; he says the songs of the black farmhands were a strong influence on his later musical direction.

Phillips started his career in Alabama, beginning as a disc jockey in 1942 at station WLAY in Muscle Shoals. He has been inducted into the **Alabama Music Hall of Fame**, which is located in Tuscumbia.

Huntsville: Elvis's daddy, Vernon, wed Dee Stanley at the Huntsville home of her brother, Richard Neely, on July 3, 1960. Apparently Elvis was still broken up over his mom's death and disapproved of the marriage—he did not attend the ceremony.

In April 1976 another marriage of note was supposed to occur nearby. After a woman named Iladean Tribble announced her betrothal to the King, media and fans descended on the **First Baptist Church of Athens**, half an hour west of Huntsville, to witness the blessed event. Elvis never showed, and Tribble later claimed she was the victim of a hoax. Duh.

Montgomery: Hank Williams, the King of Country Music, is buried in the **Oakwood Cemetery Annex**. Like Elvis, Hank was an entertainer of mythic proportions. And he died young, as well—in the backseat of a Cadillac. Instead of inspiring a slew of imitators, however, Hank begat a loutish son, Hank "Don't Give Us a Reason" Jr.

Hank's grave is covered with artificial turf. Oakwood is at 1304 Upper Wetumpka Road, a half-mile east of the police station. After you enter the cemetery, bear right at the top of the hill; the monument is on your left.

Tuscumbia: The Alabama Music Hall of Fame, which opened in July 1990, has on display the original contract between Alabaman Sam Phillips, Elvis, and RCA, whereby Phillips sold Elvis's contract to RCA for $40,000, including a $5,000 bonus for Elvis. It's signed by Elvis, Vernon, Phillips, Colonel Parker (Elvis's newly installed manager), and the RCA suits. There are also exhibits on Hank Williams, Jim Nabors—including his Gomer Pyle and Las Vegas outfits—and other Alabama-bred music figures.

The Hall, on U.S. 72, is open Monday–Saturday, 10:00 A.M.–6:00 P.M.; Sunday, 1:00 P.M.–5:00 P.M. Admission: $6 adults, $5 seniors and students, $3 kids 6–12. Info: (205) 381-4417.

ARIZONA

Phoenix: Elvis's concert of September 9, 1970, at the **Veterans Memorial Coliseum** was filmed for *Elvis—That's the Way It Is*. It was the kickoff concert for his first tour since the 1950s. Elvis's rendition here of "Mystery Train"/"Tiger Man" is seen in the film. In an odd gesture, at the end of the show Elvis tossed his scarf not to the audience but to Colonel Parker. Elvis also began a 1973 tour at the Coliseum, the home of the Phoenix Suns basketball team. The Coliseum is located at 1826 West McDowell. Program info: (602) 252-6771.

Sedona: *Stay Away, Joe* was filmed in and around this crystal-crazed New Age haven in October 1967. The decrepit house seen in the film was constructed in the foothills, with the area's scenic red rocks as a backdrop. Some shooting was also done in Cottonwood, about 20 miles southwest of Sedona.

ARKANSAS

Elvis did a lot of touring here in 1955 to cash in on his "Louisiana Hayride" appearances: the broadcasts reached northwestern Louisiana, eastern Texas, and southern Arkansas.

Bono: A September 1955 Elvis concert here drew 1,152 people, effecting a Woodstock-like impact on this town of 311 residents.

Delight: This is the hometown of Glen Campbell, who played and sang on the *Viva Las Vegas* sound track and wrote three tunes that Elvis sang: "Gentle on My Mind," "Turn Around, Look At Me," and "By the Time I Get to Phoenix." Campbell and Elvis were amigos; Elvis occasionally imitated him in concert. ("Hey, ever'body, ahm Glain Caimbull.") Unfortunately, this tiny town has no tangible remembrances of the Rhinestone Cowboy.

Fort Chaffee: Elvis underwent the Haircut Heard 'Round the World here soon after his induction into the army. "Hair today, gone tomorrow" was his prepared quip. The priceless filaments were swept into a pile with those of other recruits to discourage souvenir seekers. The whole process, orchestrated by the Colonel, received inordinate media attention.

Hope: In June 1955, Elvis was driving on Highway 67 between Hope and Texarkana when his car caught fire and burned up; he and his date were OK. Three months later, he had *another* accident near Texarkana.

Hot Springs: The Bath House Show, a two-hour, family-music-and-comedy extravaganza that highlights "the history of Hot Springs music," presents both a male Mama Cass impersonator and **The Prince, Buford Pres-**

ley. Buford says that he's "the second cousin twice re-moved of a guy who once took out Elvis's garbage" and that his intent is "to do a good impersonation of a bad Elvis impersonator." He wears his pants below his belly, so that the label on his underwear shows: BUFORD, it says.

701 Central Avenue. Shows March–December; dates vary. Showtime 8:00 P.M. Info: (501) 623-1415. Adults $7.50, oldsters $7.00, kids $3.75.

This crumbling but gracious old spa, a former haunt of big-shot politicos and celebs, is home to the Mountain Valley Spring Water company, which bottles the favorite libation of both Elvis and the Colonel, who calls it "Arkansas champagne." The Colonel would promise to send business associates champagne, then deliver this water instead. Ha! Elvis stockpiled the stuff; one of his many cases is exhibited at a Graceland museum. The **Mountain Valley Visitors Center's Hall of Fame** displays photos of the water's celebrity adherents, including William Shatner, Rodney Dangerfield, Secretariat, Charo, Tiny Tim, and, yes, Elvis (positioned between non-Hall of Fame shortstop Phil Rizzuto and colorful casino czar Jack Binion). 150 Central Avenue.

Kingsland: J. R. "Johnny" Cash, one of Elvis's Sun Records contemporaries, was born in this small town in 1932. Although his birth house has been torn down, a park in the center of town honors the Man in Black with a brass plaque and concrete guitars, all surrounded by a chain-link fence.

Marianna: In June 1955 you could still see a concert bill of Elvis, Johnny Cash, and Carl Perkins. And here's one of the lucky places you could see it.

Texarkana: Colonel Parker first laid eyes on Elvis during a matinee concert performance at the Arkansas Municipal Auditorium in the spring of 1955.

CALIFORNIA (NORTHERN)

Redding: From the annals of Elvis Mania: In October 1956, a KSDA disc jockey played "Hound Dog" hour after hour at various speeds. Police were called in out of fear that the disc jockey, who was quoted as "trying to test the general trend of intelligence," had dropped dead. He later received a death threat for "degrading Elvis." Since he was the station's general manager, the disc jockey got lots of press and kept his job. But that same week, a disc jockey at KYA, in San Francisco, violated that station's Elvis-in-the-daytime ban by spinning "Love Me Tender" 14 times in a row, also at various speeds—and lost his job.

San Jose: Elvis Mania, still going strong! The city has an **Elvis Drive**; its signs are continually stolen. At last inspection, about half were missing. The as-yet-unpilfered signs are posted about three times higher than standard street signs—they're probably the most altitudinous signs on earth.

Take Highway 101 south from downtown to the Blossom Hill Road exit. Go west about a mile to Lean Avenue. Turn south another mile to Santa Teresa Boulevard. Go west about a quarter-mile till you hit Dunn. Go south on Dunn about three blocks to Elvis Drive.

St. Helena: *Wild in the Country* was filmed around here in late 1960, as well as in the Napa Valley area and in Calistoga.

South Lake Tahoe: In May 1973, Elvis turned over a $23,000 paycheck to the coronary care unit of **Barton Memorial Hospital** in Gladys's honor. A plaque there was dedicated to Elvis in 1975 to commemorate the contribution.

COLORADO

Genoa: Wonderview Tower offers an "unusual assortment" of exhibits, including ancient fossils, an entire old dance hall, and a smattering of Elvis memorabilia, which they do not promote as heavily as they should.
I-70 exit 371. (719) 763-2309.

Vail: Elvis loved snowmobiling, but Memphis wasn't a great place for it. So in the 1970s, he would frequently winter here, sometimes bringing Lisa Marie (the girl *and* the plane). Occasionally he would go around in a ski mask to avoid recognition. He celebrated his birthday here in 1976, at which time he gave away five cars—two to a Denver policeman and his wife, one to another cop, one to a TV newsman, and one to a local doctor. The cars were bought at Kumpf Lincoln-Mercury in Denver and cost a total of $70,000.

DELAWARE

Bear: Upon hearing of Elvis's death, Colonel Parker sprang into action: he phoned Vernon to make sure he didn't do anything dumb (like give away merchandising rights), then contacted Harry "The Bear" Geissler, owner of the merchandising company **Factors Etc., Inc.** He authorized Geissler to produce Elvis merchandise, which the Bear kept on doing until the estate sued the Colonel and won back control of Elvis's name, likeness, and image. Now, the Elvis trademark is licensed to a variety of manufacturers and distributors; Factors Etc., Inc., is not among them.

Dover: In 1956, Carl Perkins, basking in the success

of "Blue Suede Shoes" and in the promise of surpassing Elvis in stardom, was en route to New York for an appearance on "The Ed Sullivan Show" when his car crashed in the Dover area. His career was derailed by the time he got out of the hospital; unlike Elvis and his triumphant return from the army, Perkins was never able to regain his luster. And to add insult to injury, most people today think of "Blue Suede Shoes" as an Elvis song.

DISTRICT OF COLUMBIA

Washington, D.C., had some significance in Elvis's life. Steve Sholes, the RCA executive who in 1955 signed Elvis, was born here in 1911. In 1980, the Library of Congress's **Archive of Folk Culture** accepted Elvis as an ethnomusical genius and now documents his career as an artist, rather than as an entertainer—one of the highest respects he has been accorded. The effort for Elvis's enshrinement was mounted by a fan, Tony Mattiaccio, who compiled a four-hour tape that documented Elvis's folk genius. You can hear this tape (and see a bunch of boring folk music stuff, too), but you have to make a reservation to visit the archive: Archive of Folk Culture, Library of Congress, Washington, D.C. 20540. It's located on the Mall. Info: (202) 707-5510.

D.C. was also the setting for one of the strangest episodes in Elvis's life. In December 1970 Elvis got in a weird mood and flew here alone, incognito, on a commercial flight. He drove to the **White House** and handed a guard a note explaining that he wanted to meet President Nixon. Amazingly, Elvis was soon summoned to 1600 Pennsylvania Avenue, where Nixon greeted him and made him an honorary federal narcotics agent. Elvis gave Nixon a gun.

Elvis stayed at the **Hotel Washington**, Room 520, registering as Jon Burrows, his frequent alias. Sam the Bellhop, who still works here, knew the King from previous stays and was taken into his confidence. Another employee tells of the time one of Elvis's bodyguards went underdressed to the hotel's swanky restaurant and was denied admission. When Elvis found out about the incident he immediately checked his entire entourage out and never returned.

Hotel Washington is located at 515 15th Street NW, between Pennsylvania Avenue and F Street. Res.: (202) 638-5900. Room 520 rents for around $400 a night. And you still need to wear a shirt and shoes to get into the restaurant.

FLORIDA

Buena Vista: Elvis has been nominated for "Person of the Century" honors in the entertainment category by 2,700 universities worldwide. You can place your vote at a polling booth in **EPCOT Center**—the only catch is you first have to pay the big bucks to get into the park. Unfortunately, you cannot mail in an absentee ballot.

Crystal River: This Sun Coast town was a location for *Follow That Dream*, which was also filmed in Tampa, Ocala (the bank that Floyd the Barber thinks Elvis is robbing), Yankeetown, Inverness (the interior of the courthouse for the climactic trial), and Bird Creek. During filming, Elvis stayed at the **Port Paradise Resort** in Crystal River. 1610 Southeast Paradise Circle. Res.: (904) 795-3111.

Fort Lauderdale: After Elvis's death, the *Lisa Marie* was housed at **Executive Airport**. In February 1984 it was towed to **Fort Lauderdale Airport** and flown back to Graceland for display.

Aaron, a "country-boy shelf sitter," on sale at Lady Di's in Fort Myers.

Fort Myers: Lady Di's Collectable Boutique is the only place you can buy Aaron, a doll based on the famous photo of Elvis at age three. The signed, numbered, and dated "country-boy shelf sitter" costs $29.95. You can also get pillows with the Aaron image for $10.95. Lady Di's stocks a quantity of rare Elvis records, books, and souvenirs as well.

1064 North Tamiami Trail, North Fort Myers, Florida 33903. (813) 656-3800.

Hollywood: The train Elvis took from Memphis to Miami shortly after his release from the army was pelted with eggs here. He was en route to the filming of the 1960 Frank Sinatra–Timex TV special.

Elvis toured relentlessly the first half of 1977, and this is where he did his first show of the year, on February 12, at the Sportatorium. He had slimmed down strikingly in the few months since his last 1976 tour.

Jacksonville: It was here in May 1955 that, for the first time, concertgoers went totally bananas over Elvis, ripping his clothes off. Later that year he prompted another riot at the **Gator Bowl**. Andy Griffith was on the bill of that second show. (Griffith also costarred on TV with Elvis on the memorable 1956 "Steve Allen Show" in which Elvis wore a tuxedo while singing "Hound Dog" to a basset hound.)

Kenansville: There used to be an actual Heartbreak Hotel here. The two-story brick inn, which opened in 1915, was on SR 523, just off U.S. 41. It's no longer in business. The song's writers, Mae Axton and Tommy Durden, lived only 150 miles away but were actually inspired by a newspaper report about a suicide. ("I walk a lonely street" was the victim's parting note.)

Kissimmee: Elvis Presley Museum: Jimmy Velvet, Elvisiana maestro extraordinaire, presents outstanding museums in Nashville and Kissimmee. Items on display here include Elvis's gold-plated Beretta, his Exxon and American Express cards, three cars, a piano from Graceland, and furniture from Elvis's Beverly Hills place. In the gift shop, you might still be able to purchase copies of Elvis's death certificate.

5770 Highway 192 (2½ miles east of Disney World), in the Old Town mall. Open 10:00 A.M.–10:00 P.M. daily. Admission $4 adults, $3 kids 8–12, under 8 free. (407) 396-8594.

Miami: The fourth Frank Sinatra–Timex TV special, known as "Welcome Home, Elvis," was filmed March 1960 in the Grand Ballroom of the Fontainebleau Hotel (now the **Fontainebleau Hilton**). In a nice turnabout, Elvis sang "Witchcraft" and Sinatra sang "Love Me Tender." Within the year, goons would be threatening Elvis's life over his affair with Juliet Prowse—Elvis's *G.I. Blues* costar and evidently Sinatra's personal property.

4441 Collins Avenue, (305) 538-2000. Res.: (800) HILTONS.

Exterior shots for *Clambake* were filmed in Miami, including the Orange Bowl Regatta powerboat race in **Marine Stadium**. But Elvis never made the trip out; a double was used on location.

Pensacola: Fort Barrancas, southwest of town, is where illegal immigrant Andreas Cornelius van Kuijk (later to become Colonel Tom Parker) served in the army after a stint in Hawaii. It's here that he picked up the Southern portion of his hard-to-place accent.

Pensacola is also the hometown of Michael Edwards, Priscilla's male-model boyfriend of too many years. His book on their affair, *Priscilla, Elvis and Me*, is, next to Albert Goldman's factually fractured biographical assassination, the scummiest Elvis book ever written. In my opinion.

The book, a deluded rant on Edwards's own wonderfulness (despite the title, it has nothing at all to do with Elvis), betrays his utter soullessness. Edwards applauds himself as a wine connoisseur because he guzzles several $100 bottles a day. He lusts for 12-year-old Lisa Marie in a manner that, despite being totally sexual and depraved, he considers pure and beautiful.

St. Petersburg Beach: The **London Wax Museum** affords you the chance to see a wax Elvis. It's so realistic, so lifelike, you'll forget you're in a wax museum and will think you've stumbled backstage at the Las Vegas Hilton and will grab "Elvis" just as one of the Guys (Elvis's beefy entourage), maybe Red West, hurls you to the ground, and then you'll come to your senses and realize it is not Red but a museum employee who has you in a choke grip. 5505 Gulf Boulevard, (813) 360-6985.

Tampa: Colonel Parker made Tampa his home base back when he was a circus promoter. During the war, he served as the Tampa dogcatcher to reap the job's material advantages, such as additional rations. He founded a for-profit pet cemetery behind the **Humane Society shelter**

at 3607 Armenia Avenue. The property is now for sale; a spokesperson assures us that the animal remains have been moved.

Zephyrhills: Kathy and John Ferguson are mounting a campaign for a National Elvis Day, January 8. Over a dozen states have agreed to the designation. If you want to help the cause, send $1.50 in postage to receive info. 6010 18th Street, Zephyrhills, Florida 33540.

GEORGIA

Dunnan Presley, Elvis's great-great-great-grandfather, moved to Georgia from North Carolina in 1836. He never amassed much of a fortune and moved to Polk County, Tennessee, after a short time. John Smith, Elvis's maternal great-great-grandfather, lived in Atlanta.

Atlanta: At **Fort McPherson**, on the south end of town, Andreas Cornelius van Kuijk (Colonel Parker) enlisted in the army.

Summerville: Octogenarian Reverend Howard Finster, one of America's preeminent folk artists, considers Elvis—and himself—to be a messenger of God; his popular painted cutouts of Elvis at three, a symbol of absolute divinity, are in collections and galleries all over the world. ("Elvis at three/Is an angel to me" writes Finster.) Some versions of the cutout even bestow wings on little Elvis. You can buy one by visiting Finster at his **Paradise Gardens**. There's a minigallery of his prodigious output on the premises. Turn east off Highway 27 at Jim's Auto Parts, a powder-blue building north of the town center.

Folk artist Elayne Goodman, of Columbus, Mississippi, a mere quintagenerian, has also been dabbing that Elvis musk behind her figurative ears of inspiration. Her elaborate collages have sold for as much as 15 grand in

Rev. Howard Finster, fave folk artist of hepcats galore, chills with his posse of Little Elvi.

Rev. Howard Finster's Paradise Gardens, a veritable Little Elvis factory.

New York galleries. Will she elbow out the Reverend as the Elvis-tinged folk artist of choice amongst the fickle Trendy Artmonger set? Don't ask me, I'm just a book you bought.

HAWAII

Except during his army days, Elvis never ventured outside the U.S.A.: the farthest he ever got from the mainland was on his jaunts to Hawaii for business and pleasure. He performed two milestone concerts here: a 1961 benefit for the USS *Arizona* memorial (his last performance for eight years), and the 1973 "Elvis: Aloha from Hawaii" TV special that was beamed by satellite around the world. And unlike some of his other "travelogue" films, Elvis's three Hawaiian films (*Blue Hawaii*; *Paradise, Hawaiian Style*; and *Girls! Girls! Girls!*) were graced with Elvis's in-the-flesh, on-location presence.

Fort Shafter: At **Schofield Barracks**, three miles northwest of Honolulu, Andreas Cornelius van Kuijk (Colonel Parker) served in the army's 64th Regiment (antiaircraft), under a Captain Thomas Parker, who later rose to the rank of lieutenant colonel. It is deduced that this is where van Kuijk got the name he would later assume as a circus promoter and, eventually, the world's best-known talent manager.

Elvis performed for the troops in Schofield Barracks on his first trip to Hawaii, November 1957.

Honolulu: The **Honolulu International Center Arena** was the site of Elvis's global "Aloha" concert on January 14, 1973. After the show, the exhausted Elvis slept for 24 straight hours.

In 1968 Elvis and Priscilla attended a karate tournament here; it was then that Priscilla first laid eyes on Mike Stone, for whom she would eventually dump Elvis.

Elvis's hotel of choice in Honolulu was the **Hilton Hawaiian Village**. He stayed here while performing locally, while on vacation, and during filming. He occupied Room 14A while on tour in November 1957, returned in March 1961 for the USS *Arizona* benefit concert, and is seen arriving here by helicopter in the 1973 "Aloha" special. On vacation in May 1972 he stayed in the hotel's Rainbow Towers with Priscilla, Lisa Marie, and the entourage. In November of that year he stayed in the penthouse of the Rainbow Towers and held a press conference in the hotel's Rainbow Rib Room. His March 1977 visit, with 37 of his closest friends, was the last idyllic interlude of his life.

Nowadays, Don Ho holds forth in the hotel's domed showroom. 1005 Kalia Road, (808) 949-4321. Res.: (800) HILTONS.

Take the Elvis Elevator up to **Elvis Elvis Elvis, the All Elvis Shop** for fulfillment of your every Elvis need when in paradise. It's run by Pete Pete Pete Hernandez, who was inspired by a Michael Jackson store he saw in Japan. The fare is standard Graceland objects plus vintage souvenirs; Hernandez even possesses four bottles of Always Elvis wine. Many items are Hawaiian-ized: they'll say something like "Aloha, Elvis" or "Aloha from Hawaii."

International Marketplace, 2330 Kalakaua. (808) 923-5847 [that's (808) 92-ELVIS].

Pete's four-year-old son, **Bruno**, dons a white jumpsuit and impersonates Elvis nightly, Monday through Saturday, at the **Sheraton Waikiki Hotel**. He's on for 20 minutes of a 90-minute show called "Love Notes: 1950's Oldies But Goodies." Bruno, who started impersonating Elvis when he was three and first performed onstage at four, replaced his uncle, who used to be Elvis in the show. Info: (808) 922-4422.

Laie: You can visit the **Polynesian Cultural Center**, which was the main location for *Paradise, Hawaiian Style*: here Elvis performs in the "canoeing" number early on

Rock-a-hula, baby! Pete Hernandez, father of a four-year-old Elvis impersonator, runs this shop in Honolulu.

and later in the film's climax. The center, a full-blown tourist attraction, offers food—"Pu pu platter, my dear?"—music, and dancing, suggesting an old Kellogg's Puffa Puffa Rice commercial. West of Highway 83.

Pearl Harbor: Bloch Arena, a gymnasium on the Pearl Harbor naval base, was the site of a March 25, 1961, benefit concert—Elvis's longest show ever—that raised a crucial $65,000 for the **USS** *Arizona* **memorial**. (The *Arizona* was one of the battleships sunk by the Japanese at Pearl Harbor on December 7, 1941.) During shooting of *Paradise, Hawaiian Style*, Elvis visited the memorial.

A *Roadside Elvis* hue and cry erupted in 1980 when a proclamation at the memorial listing Elvis as a major contributor was removed—it was a day that shall live in infamy. Although a San Jose, California, fan club has installed a plaque in Bloch Arena—incorporating a photo of a dazed, stubbled King—this is not readily apparent to the general public; the other, more accessible honor *must* be restored. To learn how you can get Elvis his due, send a self-addressed, stamped envelope to Charlie Ross, Elvis Memorial Fan Club of Hawaii, P.O. Box 15120, Honolulu, Hawaii 98615.

The *Arizona* memorial is in Kewalo Basin. Open Tuesday–Sunday. Info: (808) 471-3901.

Waikiki: Elvis, Priscilla, and the Guys stayed at the **Ilikai Hotel** on several occasions. They hung out with Tom Jones, who was singing at the Ilikai in the Pacific Ballroom, on a 1969 trip. In 1966 Elvis stayed here, in Suite 2225, for six weeks while filming *Paradise, Hawaiian Style.* He often stayed in Suite 2426, taking the entire 24th floor for his entourage.

1777 Ala Moana Boulevard. Res.: (800) 367-8434. Suite 2426 has two bedrooms and an ocean view and costs $450 a night.

HAWAIIAN MOVIE LOCATIONS

OAHU

Blue Hawaii: Waikiki Beach, Ala Wai Yacht Harbor, Honolulu International Airport, the Honolulu Police Department Jail, the Punchbowl, Ala Moana Park, Hanauma Bay, Tantalus, and the Waiola Tea Room.

Paradise, Hawaiian Style: Hanauma Bay (helicopter rescue), Chinaman's Hat, Honolulu.

Girls! Girls! Girls!: Ala Wai Yacht Harbor and the Bumble Bee Tuna canning plant at Kewalo Basin. Both are near Waikiki Beach. (There was also some shooting at Milolii, on the Kona Coast of Hawaii.)

KAUAI

Blue Hawaii: Kauai Airport, Anahola, Coco Palms Resort Hotel (the wedding scene), Lydgate Park, Wailua River. Elvis stayed in the bridal suite of the Coco Palms Hotel.

Paradise, Hawaiian Style: At the Hanalei Plantation Resort, now called the Hanalei Bay Colony Resort, Elvis drops off the alligator-shoe salesman and performs a duet with Lani in the Piki Niki Lounge.

MAUI

Paradise, Hawaiian Style: Elvis mistakenly drops off the alligator-shoe salesman at the Maui Sheraton Hotel, where the endangered-species exploiter encounters an ASPCA convention.

ILLINOIS

Chicago: Each year at Christmastime, the **World Tattoo Gallery** presents an exhibit of Elvis-oriented art that is highlighted by an undraping of the world's largest black-velvet Elvis painting—it's nine feet by nine feet. Some of the art is for sale. 1255 South Wabash Street, third floor north. Call for exhibition dates. (312) 939-2222.

In July 1990 the first annual **Elvis Presley Impersonators International Association Convention** was held at the Sheraton Rosemont, 6810 North Mannheim Road. The event was unsanctioned by Graceland. To see if they'll do it again, call (708) 297-1234.

INDIANA

Elkhart: Luther Roberts's Van Man, Inc., customized a Dodge van for Elvis after he saw Conway Twitty's and had to have one, too. The company is no longer in business in Elkhart.

Indianapolis: Market Square Arena, on Market Street between Alabama and New Jersey, was the site of Elvis's final concert, a 45-minute show before 18,000 fans on June 26, 1977. He rested before the show at the Stouffer's Indianapolis Inn, probably the last rented room of his life.

Jasonville: Since January 1988, the mayor of this small town (pop. 2,500) has been an Elvis impersonator, 32-year-old **Bruce Borders**. His slogan: "By day the

"By day the mayor, by night the King." Elvoid Bruce Borders has found a new place to dwell—City Hall.

mayor, by night the King." Borders does about 55 shows a year, playing fairs, festivals, and country clubs. He started being Elvis in high school in 1975, emulating the King's early-seventies Vegas look. His stage wardrobe includes an exact replica of the 1971 Starburst suit and a copy of the Eagle Tour suit.

By day, you can catch his act at Jasonville City Hall.

IOWA

Shenandoah: This small town in the southwestern corner of the state is where the Blackwood Brothers, a gospel group that figured prominently in Elvis's life, honed their act before breaking through in Memphis. It's not much, but *you* try to find something Elvis in Iowa.

KENTUCKY

Louisville: When Grandpa Jessie Presley left Elvis's grandmother, he moved here, worked as a night watchman, remarried, and restored the extra *s* to his name to regain the ancestral spelling, Pressley. But when Elvis became famous, Jessie dropped the extra *s* so that people would know who he was. Jessie, a certified "character," recorded a single to cash in on his grandson's fame: "Billy Goat Song" b/w "Swinging in the Orchard."

In November 1956, while in town to do a concert at the Armory, Elvis had lunch with Jessie and gave him a car, a TV, and $100. (For this show, the chief of police issued a "no wiggle" warning to Elvis.) Elvis stayed at the Seal Bark Hotel that night. In 1971, when he performed at the **State Fair and Expo Center's Freedom Hall**, Elvis had the houselights turned up to greet his rascally grandpa. Jessie died in 1973.

Rosine: Bill Monroe, the Father of Bluegrass, was born here. He was not only a musical influence on Elvis, but he also wrote the flip side of Elvis's first single, "Blue Moon of Kentucky."

LOUISIANA

Bossier City: Elvis stayed at the now-defunct Al-Ida Motel when performing on "The Louisiana Hayride" radio show. Elvis liked to party in those days, and Bossier was the Sin City adjunct of Shreveport, just across the Red River. Later, when he did his final "Hayride" in 1956, Elvis stayed at the since-demolished Captain Shreve hotel in Shreveport.

Ferriday: Ferriday is best known as the home of Jerry Lee Lewis, the one rocker who might have surpassed the King while he was away in the army. His sister's **Frankie Jean's Pik Quik** drive-thru grocery is on SR 15, west of downtown, across from Taunton's Ferriday Superette. The tunnel-like store can accommodate three cars at once; you call out your grocery order and the items are fetched as you wait inside your car. Frankie Jean says she does not display her Jerry Lee memorabilia in the store for legal reasons.

New Orleans: Elvis first tried to conquer New Orleans in 1954; he was rejected by the owner of the now-defunct Cadillac Club because he was unknown. Four years later, he returned in triumph to film *King Creole*, one of his best movies. Locations included the **Vieux Carre Saloon**, **Lake Pontchartrain**, and a local high school (where Elvis is dropped off by a plastered and amorous Carolyn Jones). Elvis stayed on the 10th floor of the Roosevelt Hotel during filming. It's now the **Fairmont Hotel**, on University Place. Res.: (504) 529-7111. Suites start at over $300.

Finally, a New Orleans legend states that six girls once bound and gagged an elevator operator and held Elvis prisoner between floors for an hour. The hotel and date are never specified.

Shreveport: The 3,500-seat **Municipal Auditorium**, on Milam Street, west of Line Avenue, is where Elvis's career kicked into high gear. "The Louisiana Hayride" was broadcast weekly from here over KWKH radio; Elvis went over big in his first appearance, in October 1954—in contrast to his Grand Ole Opry debacle just weeks earlier. The "Hayride" also helped Hank Williams, Jim Reeves, Red Sovine, and Slim Whitman get started.

Elvis later appeared on the "Hayride" TV show, March 5, 1955—his TV debut. His last "Hayride" appearance was in December 1956 for a YMCA benefit at the **fairgrounds**, on Greenwood Road between Jewella and Hearne Avenues.

Shreveport is the hometown of James Burton, the former lead guitarist for Rick Nelson who joined Elvis's TCB band for the 1969 Vegas gig. Burton also plays on Elvis Costello's *King of America* album, along with fellow TCB'ers Ronnie Tutt (drums) and Jerry Scheff (guitar).

MAINE

Portland: The opening scene of the documentary *This Is Elvis* shows workers setting up for an Elvis concert at the **Cumberland County Civic Center**, 1 Civic Center Square. The date is August 16, 1977—the darkest day in history. This would have been the site of Elvis's next concert. Colonel Parker was staying at the Dunfey

Sheraton hotel here when he heard the news, and with the phones in his makeshift office he immediately sewed up merchandizing rights to the King.

MARYLAND

Baltimore: During a May 1977 concert at the **Civic Center**, Elvis felt ill and walked offstage in the middle of the show; it was the first time this ever happened. He returned after a half hour, quipping with aplomb, "Hey, when ya gotta go, ya gotta go." 201 West Baltimore Street.

Baltimore is the 1933 birthplace of Jerry Leiber, the cocomposer of "Jailhouse Rock," "Treat Me Nice," "Hound Dog," "She's Not You," and other great Elvis songs.

An Elvis commemoration, complete with impersonators, goes down here every August 16 in Broadway Market Square. Info: Office of Adventures and Fun, Recreation Pier, 1715 Thames Street, Baltimore, MD 21231.

MASSACHUSETTS

Boston: Since 1988, 25-year-old disc jockey Jay Gordon has hosted a weekly **"Elvis Only"** hour of music and Elvis talk on WODS, Oldies 103 FM. It's broadcast Sunday mornings at 8:00 A.M. Gordon, a sincere fan, is also spearheading a wing of the Elvis stamp forces, using his radio power for good, not just to get himself some cheap notoriety.

In 1975 Elvis's dog Getlo was treated by doctors on a house call at the **Copley Plaza Hotel**. Getlo died a few months after returning to Graceland. The hotel's at 138 St. James Avenue. Res.: (800) 225-7654.

MICHIGAN

Paw Paw: Frontenac Vineyards produced 120,000 bottles of Always Elvis white wine soon after his death; the Colonel waxed poetic on the back label. Elvis hated wine. Frontenac no longer bottles the stuff.

Pontiac: The Silverdome was the site of a 1975 Elvis New Year's Eve concert that set a one-shot ticket-income record: $816,000. Elvis ripped his pants in mid-performance and had to change them. Opdyke Road at SR 59; I-75 exit 77.

MISSOURI

Elvis's great-great-grandfather Dunnan Presley, Jr., ditched his wife Martha and daughter Rosella in Fulton, Mississippi, and resettled in Brown County, Missouri, with a new wife. Dunnan died here in 1900.

Charleston: Wallace Reeve's **Boomland**, a fireworks emporium cum souvenir department store, displays a 1974 and a 1975 Lincoln Continental Mark IV, one of which was Elvis's, the other, girlfriend Linda Thompson's. There's also a cream-colored 1976 Cadillac Elvis had bought for a Denver policeman. The cars, bought from a collector in town, are in Boomland's Elvis Room (admission $1). The Elvis Mark IV has a sign on it: "If U Toucha My Car, I Breaka U Face." Ha! You can buy Elvis clocks (about 40 bucks) and the Elvis Welcomes You to His World board game ($9.95) here. Boomland is at I-57 exit 10; watch for the billboards. (314) 683-6108.

De Soto: De Soto, the population center of the United States, was the hometown of Benjamin Francis "Whitey" Ford, the Duke of Paducah, who helped convince Vernon and Gladys to let Elvis sign with the Colonel.

St. Louis: Every year since 1985, an Elvis Presley Birthday Party has been held on January 8 at the **Blueberry Hill** restaurant; it's now the largest such gathering outside of Memphis, with about 600 celebrants. Your host is Blueberry Hill's owner, Joe Edwards.

The restaurant, a rock & roll Shangri-la, has a permanent Elvis Room. Inside is a 24-foot-long display case with all five original Sun records and other early collectibles, band members' shirts, and menus from Las Vegas hotels where Elvis stayed. *Esquire* and other magazines that think it's so cool to rate everything have proclaimed the jukebox here one of the world's best. Home-brewed Rock & Roll Beer is dispensed on the premises. Chuck Berry is a regular; there's lots of his memorabilia on display.

Edwards always books "the world's fourth-best Elvis impersonator" to perform on the night of the party. Fans slice into a four-and-a-half-foot-long, guitar-shaped birthday cake and join in trivia and impersonation contests—the prizes are busts of Elvis. A radio station broadcasts live from here all night. Edwards plans to honor the 15th anniversary of Elvis's death in 1992 with a show called "From Tupelo to Graceland": there will be impersonators of Vernon, Priscilla, and Gladys, as well as of the King.

6504 Delmar. Info: (314) 727-0880. $5 cover charge.

Elvis performed the second concert on his first tour since the 1950s at **Kiel Auditorium** in September 1970. He stayed at the Chase-Park Plaza hotel and stayed there again while on tour in 1973.

Kiel Auditorium is at 1400 Market Street. The Chase-Park is now low-income housing.

Springfield: This is the hometown of the Jordanaires, Elvis's longtime backup singers. The group—Gordon Stoker, Hoyt Hawkins, Neal Matthews, and Hugh Jarrett—moved to Nashville in the early 1950s.

The last tour of Elvis's life began in Springfield on June 17, 1977, at Southwestern Missouri State University's **Hammons Center**. He stayed at the local **Howard Johnson's**, 2610 North Glenstone Avenue. Res.: (417) 866-6671.

NEBRASKA

Omaha: Elvis taped the song "My Way" here in June 1977 for his last TV special, "Elvis in Concert." Elvis was performing at the **Omaha Civic Auditorium**, 1804 Capitol Avenue—one stop on the last tour of his life. The rest of the TV show was taped in Rapid City, South Dakota. It aired after his death.

NEVADA

Reno: The immense **Harrah National Auto Museum**, at 10 Lake Street South, displays the 1973 Eldorado that Elvis gave to Kang Rhee, his karate instructor. Info and hours: (702) 333-9300. $7.50 adults, $6.50 senior citizens, $2.50 kids.

Sparks: Poke around inside the **Sierra 76 Truck Stop** and you'll find the Elvis Collection, formerly known as Guns of Elvis. Most visitors are only there to get gas, but the place has some great Elvisiana—bought from Vernon's estate in the early eighties—on display: a jewelry cabinet that includes a tigereye ring, watch, and diamonds; four .45 handguns (one of which, it is claimed, was used to shoot out a TV set); and photos. A little card tells the history of each item.

200 North McCarran Boulevard; I-80 exit 19.

Stateline: A real-estate developer claimed he was beaten by the Memphis Mafia at the Sahara Tahoe during an Elvis engagement in May 1974. When the developer couldn't get inside Elvis's private party, he turned off the power to the King's suite; the Guys didn't appreciate this. His $6 million suit against Elvis and the hotel was dismissed, but it was used as an excuse for the firing of three of the Guys, Red and Sonny West and Dave Hebler, who in response wrote the first Elvis exposé, *Elvis: What Happened?*

When Elvis performed here in 1971, in the High Sierra Room, the show's highlight was "You've Lost That Lovin' Feelin'," during which he would turn away from the audience, then spin back around . . . wearing a monkey mask. During a May 1976 concert here, Elvis again demonstrated his playful side, inviting an impersonator, Douglas Roy, onstage with him. The Sahara Tahoe is now the **Lake Tahoe Horizon**, on U.S. 50. Res.: (800) 648-3395.

NEW JERSEY

Camden: This is where an RCA pressing plant produced Elvis's discount records for the Camden label. The plant is now owned by GE.

McGuire Air Force Base: Upon his return from Germany in March 1960, Elvis landed at this central Jersey airbase next to Fort Dix during a snowstorm. He ate breakfast (scrapple and eggs) at Fort Dix; the events were documented almost as thoroughly as those of his induction two years earlier.

NEW MEXICO

Albuquerque: The April 19, 1972, concert at the now-abandoned Tingley Coliseum was the last stop of the tour from *Elvis on Tour.* Elvis met a terminally ill girl during intermission, then dedicated "You Gave Me a Mountain" to her during the second half of the show.

Carlsbad: In February 1955, the Colonel, assisting Elvis's manager, Bob Neal, got his first booking for Elvis here. Neal's days as the King's manager were numbered.

NEW YORK

Brooklyn: Priscilla Ann Wagner was born here May 24, 1945. She later took the name of her stepfather, Air Force Captain Joseph Beaulieu. Like all "service brats," she relocated several times, attending junior high in Austin, Texas, before a stint in West Germany, where she met her future husband, Elvis.

At Brooklyn's **Military Ocean Terminal** in September 1958, Elvis held a press conference before going overseas on the USS *General Randall.*

Buffalo: The concert at **Memorial Auditorium**, Main Street, on April 5, 1972, was the first of the tour seen in *Elvis on Tour.* Elvis stayed at the **Statler Hotel** then, and again while on tour in June 1976.

The Statler, 107 Delaware Avenue, is now the **Statler Towers**, a mixed-use building with no rentable rooms.

New York: At RCA Studios, 155 East 24th Street, Elvis recorded "Hound Dog" and "Don't Be Cruel" on the same day in 1956. In another session here he recorded "Blue Suede Shoes." The building is now part of Baruch College.

Elvis stayed at the **Warwick Hotel**, Room 527, in 1956 while recording songs for RCA and when making his national TV debut on the Dorsey Brothers' "Stage Show" (January) and later that year, in October, when he appeared on "The Ed Sullivan Show." 65 West 54th Street, (212) 247-2700. Room 527 costs $160–$185 per night.

Otis Blackwell made demos for Elvis and others at Charlie Brave's now-defunct Allegro Studios, which was at 1650 Broadway. Songs that came from here include "Don't Be Cruel," "All Shook Up," "Great Balls of Fire," and "Fever."

At the now-defunct Maxine Elliot Theater, on 39th Street, Elvis made his second "Sullivan" appearance, scoring colossal ratings. At the legendary (and also now-defunct) Paramount Theater, *Love Me Tender* had its world premiere November 1956. At **Madison Square Garden**, Seventh Avenue at 32nd Street, Elvis performed four hot concerts—his only public shows ever in New York City—in June 1972. And at the **Apollo Theater**, 125th Street and 8th Avenue, Elvis went to see and meet Bo Diddley while in town for the Dorsey Brothers' TV show in 1956.

NORTH CAROLINA

Asheville: While staying at the Rodeway Inn for performances at the Civic Center in July 1975, Elvis "accidentally" shot out his TV set; the bullet ricocheted and struck Dr. Nick in the chest—he was not seriously injured (and didn't press charges, natch). Unfortunately, the Rodeway Inn is no longer here.

Charlotte: The **Charlotte Motor Speedway** was the main location for *Speedway*. It was later used in *Days of Thunder* (the poor man's *Speedway*).

New Bern: In 1745, Scotsman Andrew Pressley—Elvis's great-great-great-great-great-grandfather—first settled here in America, making his living as a blacksmith. His son Andrew, Jr., was born in 1754; in 1776, Junior resettled with his bride on 150 acres in Lancaster County, South Carolina. He soon signed on as a private in the Revolutionary War, returning years later to South Carolina as a blacksmith. His son, Dunnan, eventually moved the clan back to North Carolina.

OHIO

Cincinnati: Radio station WCVG got lots of publicity when it switched to an all-Elvis format in August 1988. The first song played was "Heartbreak Hotel." But all good things come to a horrible end—in 1989, WCVG became the Business Radio Network.

Cleveland: Radio station WERE, beaming out from the future home of the Rock and Roll Hall of Fame, was probably the first Northern station to play Elvis; disc jockey Bill Randle spun one of the King's platters in January 1955.

In August of that year, Elvis appeared with Bill Haley and Pat Boone at the **St. Michael's School Assembly Hall**, 6912 Chestnut Road, and at the now-defunct Circle Theater. The shows were filmed for an unreleased Universal short subject on Randle; the footage has never surfaced. It must have been a study of contrast: Elvis was a cool white man who could sound like a cool black; Boone was a corny white man who could make really cool black music sound corny and white.

Toledo: At the **Sports Arena**, 1 Main Street, an unemployed steelworker took a swing at Elvis in November 1956 because his wife's love for the King had broken up their marriage; he had discovered a photo of Elvis, not him, in her wallet. Elvis punched back. The police later complimented Elvis on the way he handled himself.

OKLAHOMA

Sooners have an abiding love for the King, manifested by a slew of memorial plaques at venues where he appeared. There's one at **The Myriad**, in Oklahoma City (Reno Avenue, west of Robinson), where Elvis sang in 1973, 1975, and 1976. There's one at the **Mabee Center**, on the Oral Roberts University campus in Tulsa, where he performed in 1974 and on the bicentennial in 1976. There's one at the Tulsa fairgrounds, dedicated on April 21, 1991. And there's one at the **Lloyd Noble Center**, on the O.U. campus in Norman, where he appeared in 1977.

Bristow: Bill and Judy Wilson of the Oklahoma Fans for Elvis are mounting a campaign to obtain a Presidential Medal of Freedom for the King, based on his many charitable contributions and his music. Past recipients have included Frank Sinatra and Lucille Ball, so why not Elvis?

To receive an information packet, send a stamped, self-addressed envelope to Bill and Judy at 421 West Sixth Street, Bristow, Oklahoma 74010.

Oklahoma City: The National Casket Company manufactured Elvis's 900-pound seamless copper casket. The company was bought out in 1980.

OREGON

Portland: The 24-hour, coin-operated **Church of Elvis** is part of a wacky art gallery called Where's the Art!!

A couple exchanges vows at the Church of Elvis.

Images of the King—such as the Miracle of the Spinning Elvises—entice many to engage in sham wedding ceremonies, confessions, and catechisms here to the sounds of "Love Me Tender." There's even been a *real* wedding here of a Chicago couple who won the ceremony in a radio contest.

Owner Stephanie Pierce quit her job as an East Coast lawyer, moved to Oregon, and pursues her muse. Her slogan: "Twenty-four hours, twenty-five cents."

219 SW Ankeny Street. Open 24 hours. 25 cents.

U.S.A.

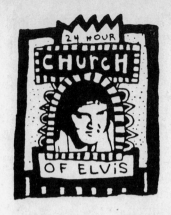

The Church of Elvis:
24 hours, 25 cents.

Redmond: The Fantastic Museum owns Elvis's first guitar, which he bought at Tupelo Hardware. The museum, which *is* truly fantastic, also has Olaf (a nine-foot mummified giant), antique outhouses, Ike's inauguration Caddy, Liz Taylor's trailer, Bing Crosby's fishing rods and muddy boots, and miniature houses built by a one-handed blind man. The museum is currently closed, but its owner has high hopes to reopen it soon. Call Redmond info, (503) 555-1212, to see if it's back in business.

PENNSYLVANIA

Chester: His hometown is now a depressing slum, but on the sidewalk outside rock pioneer Bill Haley's demolished **boyhood home**, at Fifth and Crosby, are musical notes (representing the Comets) and a star (Haley).

Levittown: Memphis Memories, an all-Elvis store, is run by Linda and "Rockin'" Ron Cade. (Cade also hosts an all-Elvis radio show—see Philadelphia.) The store sells records, memorabilia, and the occasional vintage souvenir.

Open Tuesday–Thursday, noon–6:00 P.M.; Friday, 11:00 A.M.–9:00 P.M.; Saturday, 10:00 A.M.–9:00 P.M.; Sunday, 10:00 A.M.–6:00 P.M. You can get a mail-order catalog for $2. Write to: Memphis Memories, 4017 Route 413, Levittown, Pennsylvania 19056. (215) 943-4089.

Nanticoke: Nick Adams, Elvis's only Hollywood pal, was born Nicholas Adamshock here in 1931. Before budding up to Elvis, Adams had been James Dean's pal; Elvis thought that made Adams really cool.

Philadelphia: Rockin' Ron Cade hosts the **"Elvis & Friends Radio Show"** every Sunday morning from 8:00 A.M. till 10:00 A.M. on WOGL, 1210 AM and 98.1 FM. The program, which has been on the air since the late seventies, features a mix of talk, interviews, and music.

Pittsburgh: Elvis appeared in June 1973 and on New Year's Eve 1976 at the **Pittsburgh Civic Arena**. Vernon, Lisa Marie, and girlfriend Ginger Alden were at the New Year's show, which was, by all accounts, outstanding. To commemorate these dates, a group of fans raised funds for a plaque, which was dedicated January 8, 1982. It features Elvis's profile in bronze and the lightning-bolt TCB and TLC logos.

Elvis in Pittsburgh: A pair of one-night stands, a lifetime of memories.

The plaque is located inside the Arena, near Gate 1. If you ask, a guard will take you to see it. Auditorium Place, (412) 642-1800.

Ridgway: Elvis's Dr. Nick (George Constantine Nichopoulos) was born here in 1927; his family moved to Anniston, Alabama, shortly thereafter.

SOUTH CAROLINA

Lancaster County: Elvis's great-great-great-great-grandparents Elizabeth and Andrew Presley, Jr., lived here after the Revolutionary War; Andrew worked as a blacksmith, like his father. Their vagabond son, Dunnan, moved to North Carolina when he was 20 and fathered seven children with two wives.

SOUTH DAKOTA

Murdo: In 1980 the **Murdo Pioneer Auto Museum** swapped a huge 1932 Packard Phaeton for a 1976 Harley motorcycle that had been owned by the King. Despite constant offers from the Japanese, the cycle remains the centerpiece of this 280-car collection, which also includes a Tucker and a 1921 motor home. On display are copies of the title to the bike—still registered to Elvis A. Presley—along with posters and pictures, including one on a slab of wood. Owner Dave Geisler loves Elvis; the King's spiritual songs are piped in at the display.

I-90 exit 192; 503 Fifth Street, behind the Hallmark Store. Open April–November. Summer hours: 7:00 A.M.–10:00 P.M. daily. (605) 669-2691.

Elvis's Harley, Murdo, South Dakota. It ain't for sale.

Rapid City: Rushmore Plaza Civic Center, 444 Mt. Rushmore Road North, is where most of Elvis's last TV special, "Elvis in Concert," was taped for CBS. It was recorded in June 1977 during the last tour of his life, and aired after his death. He stayed at the **Holiday Inn**, 1902 LaCrosse Street. Res.: (605) 348-1230.

TEXAS

Abilene: Dennis Linde, who composed and played gitbox on Elvis's last big hit, "Burning Love," hails from Abilene.

Austin: The Beaulieu family lived in 1956 at Bergstrom Air Force Base, just before moving to Germany.

When Priscilla first heard of Elvis, she was Class Queen at Del Valley Junior High (now **Del Valley Middle School**), 12712 Pearce Lane.

Dallas: Dallas is a city of Elvis firsts: the first Elvis fan club was started here. Colonel Parker made his first move on Elvis at the **Sportatorium**, 1000 South Industrial, during the Big D Jamboree of June 1955. And **Big State Record Distributors**, still in business, was the first company to place a large order for an Elvis record, requesting several hundred copies of "That's All Right (Mama)"/"Blue Moon of Kentucky."

Fort Hood: Elvis was stationed here in 1958. He was assigned to A Company, Second Medium Tank Battalion, Second Armored Division. Ironically, this is where Lieutenant Colonel Thomas Parker (whose name Elvis's Colonel appropriated) was killed in an accident in 1945. Elvis rented a house in nearby Killeen so his parents could be near him during his stint.

Fort Worth: The *Lisa Marie* was refurbished here to Elvis's specifications, setting him back more than $846,000. Elvis liked to come down here with friends to observe the progress on his toy of toys.

Gladewater: In August 1954 Elvis, Scotty Moore, and Bill Black made their first-ever out-of-town appearance here.

Hillsboro: Elvis's bus made a lunch stop here on the way to Fort Hood from Fort Chaffee, Arkansas, in March 1958 in order to foil fans and press who were waiting at the usual stop in Waxahachie.

Houston: Elvis gave several self-confidence-building performances in Houston through the years. He, Scotty, and Bill made one of their first out-of-town appearances at **Magnolia Gardens**, 12044 Beach, in August 1954. They also played time and again at the **Eagles' Hall**, run by the Fraternal Order of the Eagle.

Elvis's first non-Vegas performances since the early sixties were six supersuccessful concerts at the **Astrodome** (Kirby Drive at I-610) in February and March 1970. He entered in a red jeep and at the finale of each show tooled around the dome in it. In March 1974 he did two shows in the dome in one day, generating much cash flow.

Killeen: Beginning June 1958, Vernon and Gladys lived here in a rented four-bedroom bungalow—at an extortionate $1,400 per month—while Elvis was stationed at Fort Hood. Gladys became fatally ill while living here, and Elvis sent her to Methodist Hospital in Memphis.

Lubbock: The town's **Walk of Fame** honors Mac Davis—whose Elvis-recorded songs include "In the Ghetto," "Memories," and "Don't Cry Daddy"—and Buddy Holly. It's at 8th Street and Avenue Q. Other **Buddy Holly remembrances** include an eight-and-a-half-foot statue near the Walk of Fame, his grave in Lubbock Cemetery (34th Street), his birthplace (1911 Sixth Street), and his 1957 home (1305 37th Street). The town holds an annual birthday celebration, **Budfest**, in the first week of September.

Elvis played in Lubbock on a bill with a very young Buddy in October 1955, at the Cotton Club (14-year-old Mac Davis was in the audience). At the time, Buddy was part of the duo Buddy and Bob. The next day, Buddy, Bob, and Elvis performed a promotional gig at Hub Motors, an automobile dealership.

San Antonio: The Elvis concert at T. H. Barton Coliseum on April 18, 1972, included the Jackie Kahane monologue seen in *Elvis on Tour*. Kahane was chosen as Elvis's longtime warmup because his humor was clean. Kahane delivered a stand-up eulogy at Elvis's funeral.

Waco: Elvis's close friend **Eddie Fadal** has converted his home into a minimuseum to the King; it's one of the choicest stops of *Roadside Elvis*.

When Fadal met Elvis in early 1956 he was working as a disc jockey at KRLD in Dallas. In 1958, when Elvis

The house where Private Elvis took weekend retreats from basic training is now a shrine. The wing at right was added for the King.

was stationed 45 miles away at Fort Hood, he and his parents would visit Eddie's home in Waco almost every weekend. Eddie custom built a room for Elvis, decorating it in pink and black. Eddie says Waco merchants would give Elvis whatever he wanted for free, considering it an honor just to serve him. Elvis cut an album—*Forever Young, Forever Beautiful*—in the living room of Eddie's home; Eddie has movies of the sessions. If he's there, maybe you can get a private screening.

The house is now leased to some Elvis fans and is open for tours by appointment. There's a monument in the front yard by Elvis's window, a live oak with the inscription: In Memory of Elvis Presley.

Inside the house is a memorabilia room, with pajamas, a bathrobe, sweaters, shirts, photos, autographed albums, videos, concert photos, all his albums, and more. Fan clubs hold meetings here; groups from England, France, Germany, Switzerland, Sweden, and Japan have convened here.

"Many say they prefer it to Graceland," says Eddie, who moved to another house the day Elvis died.

2807 Lasker Avenue, off I-35. Call ahead, even the day of your visit, because there are no regular hours. (817) 776-5388.

The glorious stained and leaded glass at the Waco, Texas, Elvis shrine. Man, you oughta see it in color.

IN LOVING REMEMBRANCE OF
ELVIS AARON PRESLEY
1935 ⟶ 1977
"A LOVING HOME AWAY FROM HOME"
WACO, TEXAS 1956—1958

A monument at the Waco, Texas, house.

Waco is currently building a Walk of Fame along the Brazos River. Included in the Walk are Willie Nelson, Ann Sheridan, and Paul Robeson. Eddie Fadal bought a star for Elvis.

Wink: Roy Orbison, another country-rock artist who broke through on Sun Records, was born in this micropolis in 1936. His childhood home was destroyed; Wink burghers are trying to erect a statue and museum, but they *need money.*

UTAH

Salt Lake City: The University of Utah's **Center for Human Toxicology**, University at South Street, was one of three places where Elvis's blood was tested after his death.

VERMONT

North Springfield: Here you'll find the heart of the Elvis stamp movement, spearheaded by Mrs. Pat Geiger. Geiger has spent a frustrating seven years pursuing her dream: "Once Elvis's stamp is issued," she says, "I will never again put myself in the position of having to deal with such idiots."

Geiger envisions the stamp being like the portrait of Elvis done by Memphis artist John Robinette for the Elvis Presley Memorial Trauma Center in Memphis. She has fired off countless witty missives to the Postal Service idiots; she is alarmed at rumors that the Elvis stamp will not be a commemorative but an unimpressive coil stamp, or that it will be less than first-class postage.

VIRGINIA

Hampton: A 16-by-24-inch brass plaque on the west interior wall of the **Hampton Coliseum** commemorates four shows Elvis did here, one of which was filmed for *Elvis on Tour*. The Friends Thru Elvis Fan Club sold candy bars to fund the plaque, which was dedicated in 1978. It's near the junction of I-64 and I-664.

Nassawadox: Arthur "Big Boy" Crudup, who composed and recorded the song that became the A side of Elvis's first record, "That's All Right (Mama)," was born in Virginia in 1905 and died here in 1974, at North Hampton-Accomac Hospital.

More recently, Nassawadox has become the home of impersonator Clearance Giddens, who bills himself as "the Black Elvis." His fervent followers refer to themselves as Black Heads.

Richmond: At Gus Serafim's **Celebrity Room** restaurant, "where it's Christmas every day," different groups of tables are named and themed after stars, including Clark Gable, Judy Garland, Marilyn Monroe, Paul Newman, and Elizabeth Taylor. Clips and memorabilia are displayed under the glass tabletops. But the only celeb to rate a separate room is . . . that's right—Elvis.

The 50-seat Elvis Room has existed since the mid-sixties. There's a wall of albums, an Elvis shirt, photos, and more. Fan clubs hold meetings here and screen Elvis movies.

7515 Brook Road. Res.: (804) 266-3328.

Elvis stayed at the **Hotel Jefferson** while barnstorming during the magic year of 1956. Franklin and Adams Streets. Res.: (804) 788-8000.

Roanoke: Don and Kim Epperly have the world's finest homemade Elvis tribute in their front yard. A few

years back, Don built Kim an elaborate miniature Graceland, including a guitar-shaped swimming pool and a replica of Graceland's Meditation Gardens. He followed that with a waist-high facsimile of Elvis's Tupelo birthplace. Don and Kim continue to add a building a year, and now the site contains Vernon's house, a civic center called Presley Hall (where Elvis performs for an audience of Barbies), and replicas of Graceland's car museum and Heartbreak Hotel restaurant. An airport is on the way; the miniature *Lisa Marie* is all fueled up and ready to go.

Every day, Kim places an Elvis doll—dressed appropriately for the weather—somewhere in the display. And just like at the Memphis Graceland, the grounds are decked out every December for Christmas, and a candlelight service is held "on the grounds" every August 16.

The Epperly's Graceland is at 605 Riverland Road SE. Anybody's welcome to visit from 10:00 A.M. till 10:30 P.M., and there's no charge, but the Epperlys ask that you consider making a charitable donation to the organization of your choice when you get back home.

In April 1972 Elvis was handed the keys to Roanoke—Wayne Newton's hometown—by the mayor at **Woodrum Field** airport; it was filmed for *Elvis on Tour*. On tour in August 1976, he and Linda Thompson stayed at the Sheraton Inn, Suite 214–216.

The Sheraton, at 2727 Ferndale Drive NW, is now a **Quality Inn**. Res.: (703) 562-1912. Suite 214–216, at $56 a night, is one of the most affordable Elvis rooms you'll find anywhere.

WASHINGTON

Seattle: Elvis spent time here in September 1962 while filming *It Happened at the World's Fair*. Locations included the monorail, the Skyride, the Dream Car Exhibit (this is where little Sue-Lin hides out), the NASA exhibit (where Elvis goes at the end to apply for an astronaut job), the **Space Needle restaurant**, and many other exhibits. You can re-create the film's romantic dinner with your own Elvis (or nurse) at the Space Needle restaurant, in the Seattle Center. Res.: (206) 443-2100.

During filming, Elvis stayed in a 14th floor suite at the New Washington Hotel, which was torn down years ago. The site is now the Theadora House, a retirement home for Catholics.

WEST VIRGINIA

Huntington: Colonel Parker used to claim he was born in Huntington to parents in a traveling carnival, but he was *lying*. It's not Parker's illegal-immigrant status that is so objectionable. It's that Parker would not permit Elvis to cross any borders that would require a passport, thus denying Elvis a chance to tour the globe.

WISCONSIN

Manitowoc: In 1978 a local foundry worker, Herbert Baer, legally changed his name to Elvis Presley. When we called, we asked if Herbert Baer was there. "No-o-o-o-o." "Is *Elvis Presley* there?" "Y-e-e-e-e-es." Baer—sorry, *Presley*—was outraged that the media had described him as weighing 170 pounds when he actually weighed 150. A newspaper clip and a picture of "EP II" is on the bulletin board at the Manitowoc Courthouse. Baer/Presley has not attempted to exploit his new moniker; he's apparently satisfied *just being Elvis*.

2
Tupelo

Back when the infant King was belting out those diaper-rash blues in East Tupelo, the town was on the proverbial wrong side of the tracks, separated from Tupelo proper by cotton fields and, yes, train tracks. Now it's all one big happy Tupelo. The town's north-south divider is Main Street. The east-west divider is the train tracks. Most Presley residences, including Elvis's birthplace, are east of the tracks.

Elvis's dad, Vernon, was born in 1916 in Fulton, about 20 miles east of Tupelo. Besides his brother Vester, Vernon's siblings included Delta Mae, Nasval (Aunt Nash), and Gladys Earline (Little Gladys). Vester and Delta can still be found around Graceland. Vernon's mom, Minnie Mae Hood "Dodger" Presley, and dad, Jessie D. (J.D.), were also born in Fulton. J.D. and Dodger broke up: Dodger stayed with Vernon and Elvis and is buried beside them in the Meditation Garden at Graceland. J.D. moved to Louisville; Elvis would look up his prodigal grandfather whenever a tour brought him to town. J.D. died in 1973. Vernon's grandmother, Rosella

"Rosie" Presley, had 10 children but never married—so all took her surname. Rosie was born and died in Fulton.

Elvis's mom, Gladys, was born just outside Tupelo in 1912. One of her sisters, Clettes, married Vester. Their daughter, Patsy Presley Gambill—who had the genetic possibility of being a second Elvis—was part of the extended Graceland family. And one of Gladys's brothers, Travis, was the beloved gate guard at Graceland for many years. Gladys's parents, Octavia Lavinia "Doll" Mansell and Robert Lee Smith, lived their lives in the Tupelo area. They died in Spring Hill, about an hour northwest of Tupelo; Grandpa Bob was buried in an unmarked grave in Spring Hill Cemetery. Their parents, Obe and Anna Smith, lived in Saltillo, on the northern outskirts of Tupelo.

Gladys and Vernon purchased their marriage license after hitchhiking to Pontotoc, 20 miles west of Tupelo. They were married in Verona, just south of Tupelo, on June 17, 1933.

A serene route to Tupelo from the northeast (say, Nashville) or southwest (Jackson or Natchez, Mississippi)

is the Natchez Trace Parkway. Just remember to tank up before you leave; there are no services on the parkway.

Highway 78 from Memphis to Tupelo was renamed in December 1977 the Elvis Aron Presley Memorial Highway. This is most likely the route Vernon took when he uprooted the family to Memphis in 1948.

ELVIS, VERNON, AND GLADYS SLEPT HERE

The dirt-poor Presleys played musical houses in Tupelo: they frequently bunked with relatives, depending on finances. Most of the houses were within a few blocks of each other. The neighborhood is just west of Elvis's birthplace: boundaries are Reese on the north, Kelly on the south, Adams on the west, and Elvis Presley Drive, formerly Old Saltillo Road, on the east.

Specific addresses are unknown, but a stroll around the peaceful environs, minutes from the tour-bus pandemonium of the birthplace, will give you a sense of where Elvis grew up. The houses are simple, but the neighborhood is darn pleasant. Many structures remain from the Days of Elvis. In August 1979 the area was designated Presley Heights.

Gladys lived on Kelly Street while Vernon was courting her. Elvis, Gladys, and Vernon also lived on Kelly in 1942, when Elvis entered second grade. "Doll" Smith, Gladys's grandma, lived on Berry Street, and this is where Gladys and Vernon were living when Elvis and his stillborn twin Jesse were conceived. Unfortunately, nobody is telling the exact site where this momentous merging transpired—probably because too many Elvis fans would try to re-create the moment, and its results, on the spot.

Vernon, Gladys, and Elvis moved back to Doll's house

in 1943. They lived in two other houses on Berry Street over the years. In the early forties, the family also lived for a while on Reese Street with Vernon's brother, Vester. And in 1944, the family lived on Adams Street, near the First Assembly of God church.

The biggest housing crisis came in 1938, when Vernon was sentenced to three years at the frightful Parchman Farm penitentiary, in west-central Mississippi, for a minor forgery. He and his coconspirators were sentenced at the Lee County Circuit Court, on Court Street, and were temporarily incarcerated in the Lee County Jail. During Vernon's time in jail, Gladys and Elvis moved into the South Tupelo home of Gladys's cousin Frank Richards. It still stands, at 510½ Maple Street.

Things never got better for the Presleys in Tupelo. They moved to a cheaper house on Commerce Street in 1946. A forlorn shopping mall now rests on the site. Later 1946 houses included Mulberry Alley (near the fair-

Elvis and Gladys crashed at 510½ Maple Street while Vernon was in the slammer.

1010 North Green Street, the Presleys' last address in Tupelo.

grounds) and **1010 North Green Street**, in the northeast part of town. The Green Street house, their last in Tupelo, still stands.

Gladys and Elvis spent three weeks in the Tupelo Hospital charity ward, 830 South Gloster Street, after his birth. It's now called **North Mississippi Medical Center**. Which leads us to our main reason for visiting Tupelo. . . .

THE ELVIS PRESLEY BIRTHPLACE

The grounds comprise the actual house where, on January 8, 1935, Elvis was born, along with the Elvis Presley Memorial Chapel, the Elvis Presley (Youth) Center, and Elvis Presley Park.

The house is at 306 Elvis Presley Drive. Hours May–September are Monday–Saturday, 9:00 A.M.–5:30 P.M.; Sunday, 1:00 P.M.–5:00 P.M. October–April hours are Monday–Saturday, 10:00 A.M.–5:00 P.M.; Sunday, 1:00 P.M.–5:00 P.M. (601) 841-1245. Admission to the birthplace (all other attractions are free): Adults $1; kids under 12, $.50.

The coolest historical marker in America.

The shotgun shack where Elvis first hiccuped.

The House: The Elvis Presley Birthplace, open to the public since 1971, was declared a state historical monument on January 8, 1978. None of the furnishings—including, curiously, a framed copy of Rudyard Kipling's

The original pulpit from the Assembly of God church and the Presley family Bible.

poem "If"—are authentic Elvisabilia: the only original elements are the floor, walls, fireplace, door frames, and window frames. The 450-square-foot house (called a shotgun shack because, if you really wanted to, you could shoot a gun through the front door and the shot would exit out the back) was built in 1934 by Vernon on land leased from local fat cat Orville Bean.

Elvis Presley Memorial Chapel: This, the highlight of the birthplace complex, belongs to the fans. Dedicated August 17, 1979, by the Elvis Presley Memorial Commission, the $800,000 chapel—down to each stained glass panel and every pew—was funded by donations from friends and admirers. One pew comes to you courtesy of the Colonel.

As might be expected, the chapel is a popular spot for Elvis fans to wed. (Some have married in the birthplace itself.) Inside is the original pulpit from the First Assembly of God church; upon it, under glass, is Elvis's old

Can you spot the hidden Elvis in the stained glass?

Bible, donated by Vernon. Flanking the pulpit are a pair of golden vases, one donated by Billy and Jo Smith (who played racquetball with Elvis the night he died), the other by Kathy Westmoreland (one of Elvis's girlfriends and backup singers). The stands for the vases were donated by Patsy Presley Gambill and by the From The Heart Fan Club, of Huntsville, Alabama. None of the stained glass *seems* to portray a discernible Elvis image; however, if you stare at it long enough. . . .

Elvis Presley (Youth) Center: Elvis provided seed money for the center with a 1957 benefit concert in Tupelo. It now houses an extensive gift shop and "information center"; proceeds go to the Elvis Presley Memorial Foundation. The "information" is about all the stuff for sale: commemorative plates, thimbles, bells, spoons, Elvis license plates, actual copies of the *Memphis Press Scimitar* (does that town have great newspaper names or what?) of August 17, 1977, lots and lots of eight-track tapes, and leftover clothing swatches from Elvis's wardrobe that were once included in a record album. (Former secretary Becky Yancey, in her book, *My Life with Elvis*, divulges that many of the clothes were simply gifts from fans, not things he actually wore.)

The best souvenir is a postcard of the Las Vegas Hilton with a diseased poem by the Colonel on the back. Lines include: "Kissin' cousins and roustabout/And then we knew what he was all about." Not one to waste a promotional opportunity, at the bottom of the card he adds an exhortation: "The Colonel says: Visit Graceland."

Elvis Presley Park: Although possessing a perfectly fine playground, public swimming pool, small baseball field, and tennis court, Elvis Presley Park seems an unfitting tribute to the man. A proper Elvis Park should have had a racquetball court, karate mats, a go-cart course, and a shooting range.

Gladys Glen, outside the chapel. A place to reflect, to pray, to lighten your load.

ELVIS SANG HERE

Every Saturday afternoon in the forties, WELO radio would broadcast an amateur show called the "Saturday Jamboree" from the still-standing county courthouse, on Court Street between North Broadway and North Spring. By some accounts, Elvis first appeared on the Jamboree as early as age eight, singing "Old Shep," and he kept on singing "Old Shep" on Saturdays till he left Tupelo. Whatever the actual dates, WELO was surely the first station to broadcast Elvis. In 1955 Elvis, Johnny Cash, and Carl Perkins appeared on a WELO program together—yet another historic radio moment.

The studios for WELO (580 on your AM dial) were, at the time, above the Black and White Hardware Store, 212 South Spring Street. The whole block was later razed to make room for the awesomely ugly People's Bank Building. And WELO is now 58 Gold, The Home of Good-Time Rock & Roll, spinning such good-time favorites as Cat Stevens and Neil Diamond.

Besides whatever harmonizing young Elvis might have done in the classroom or in church, his public performances in Tupelo prior to stardom were almost always of "Old Shep," a slow, lamentful ditty about a boy who has to put his dog to sleep. (He recorded "Old Shep" in 1956.)

Elvis's first success before a live audience was in October 1945, at the age of ten, singing "Old Shep" at the **Tupelo fairgrounds** in a competition at the Mississippi-Alabama Fair; he took second place. (The winner, Shirley Jones Gallentine, certainly has something cool to tell her grandchildren.) He returned here September 1957 in a benefit for what would become the Elvis Presley Youth Center.

The fairgrounds are south of East Main, near Highway 45. There's an Elvis Presley Memorial Grandstand. They still hold the Mississippi-Alabama Fair here.

ELVIS LEARNED HERE

Elvis's elementary school was the East Tupelo Consolidated School System, now called the **Lawhon Elementary School**. In the fifth grade, Elvis did his first public singing in the school auditorium. That's right—"Old Shep." The Lawhon School is at 140 Lake Street, south of East Main Street.

In 1946 Elvis enrolled at **Milam Junior High School**, where he would endure sixth, seventh, and some of eighth

Elvis's junior high.

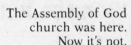

The Assembly of God
church was here.
Now it's not.

grade before the family moved to Memphis. It's at 720 West Jefferson, at the corner of Gloster.

Elvis's off-campus learning experiences in Tupelo were far more significant. At the First Assembly of God church, pastored by Reverend James Ballard, young Elvis gained an appreciation for the power of uninhibited gospel wailing. The accompaniment here was a guitar, not a piano or organ. Some say that Vernon and Gladys first met at the church, which was at 206 Adams Street, a site now occupied by the First Apostolic Church of Jesus Christ.

Young Elvis dreamt here of becoming a movie star. You can, too, but you won't become a movie star.

The other major influence on young Elvis was the movies; he would frequent the Lyric and Strand theaters whenever possible. Although the Strand is gone, the Lyric remains, at the corner of North Broadway and Court Street, across from the county courthouse.

GLADYS OR VERNON WORKED HERE

One axiom about Elvis's roots that seems to hold true is that Vernon was not too fond of working. He never stayed very long at any job; Gladys probably brought in as much income as he did.

Gladys was working at the Tupelo Garment Company as a sewing machine operator when she met Vernon and later when she got pregnant. Vernon did deliveries for Roy Martin's Groceries, Lake Street, at Highway 78 and North Saltillo Road, for a short time. Both these establishments are long gone.

After his 1939 release from the Parchman prison farm, Vernon worked for the **Leake and Goodlett** lumber yard, 105 East Main Street. The place is still there, as is **Long's Cleaners**, 130 East Main Street, where Vernon and Vester worked in the early forties. The wonderfully de-

Vernon worked at Long's Cleaners until he didn't want to anymore.

crepit sign outside probably predates even that era. It's right near the entrance to the fairgrounds.

JESSE GARON

Elvis's stillborn twin, Jesse Garon, was buried in an unmarked grave in **Priceville Cemetery**, a few miles northeast of the birthsite, on Feemster Lake Road. (Go north on Feemster Lake off Main Street.) Gladys would take young Elvis there and they would talk to Jesse. In fact, Gladys and Elvis seemed to consider Jesse their "guiding spirit." When Elvis was a bad boy, Gladys shamed him by saying that Jesse would have behaved better. (The whole Jesse-Gladys-Elvis thing should keep pointy-headed analysts stroking their goony beards for years.)

According to the Tupelo Cemetery Register, there are seven Presleys buried here, not counting Jesse. They range from Noah and Susan Griffin Presley, born in the 19th century, to Virginia Presley Shoefner, who died in

1975. Noah was Elvis's great uncle. Given the twisty, gnarled nature of the Presley family tree, all seven of the deceased are possible relations.

ELVIS'S FIRST GUITAR

Gladys bought Elvis his first guitar at George Booth's **Tupelo Hardware** in January 1946 for $7.75 (plus 2-percent sales tax). A display case here now includes clippings, photostats, and a beat-up old guitar case of no attribution. For $1.50 you can buy a guitar-shaped soft red plastic key holder that says "Tupelo Hardware: Where Elvis Bought His First Guitar."

There's a 1979 letter in the display case from Forrest L. Bobo, the clerk who waited on Gladys and Elvis, telling the story: Elvis wanted a .22 rifle, but Gladys wanted him to get a guitar. Elvis didn't have enough of his own money

Elvis bought his first guitar at a hardware store. Interestingly, many a musician refers to his instrument as his "axe."

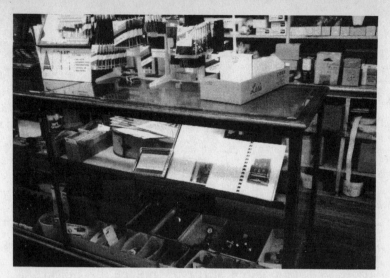

Display about Elvis's first guitar at Tupelo Hardware. Come for the display, leave with a bunch of nails, the owner figures.

to buy the guitar, so Gladys offered to make up the difference.

114 West Main Street, at North Front Street. Open Monday–Friday, 7:00 A.M.–5:30 P.M.; Saturday, 7:00 A.M.–noon. (601) 842-4637.

TUPELO SALUTES ELVIS

The impressive **Tupelo Museum** includes an actual old railroad depot, a slew of rusty old farm implements, and, in a salute to the 20th century, a Space Museum. It also has, as you might expect, a section devoted to Elvis.

Elvis newspaper clips are everywhere, the old-time movie theater is bedecked with Elvis movie posters, and the Old Town section has a re-creation of WELO Studios, including a dummy with his feet up on a desk, snoozing under a newspaper. But it's the Elvis Room, behind a glass storm door, that will set the Elvis fan's heart aflutter. Inside is a *big* replica of the birthplace, assorted ephemera including a copy of *Elvis: What Happened?*, and velvet paintings.

The Tupelo Museum is in Ballard Park, off Highway 6, west of town. It's open Tuesday–Friday, 10:00 A.M.–4:00 P.M.; Saturday and Sunday, 1:00 P.M.–5:00 P.M. Admission is $1 adults, 50¢ kids 3–12. (601) 841-6438.

RONALD McDONALD SALUTES ELVIS

The most comprehensive—and unexpected—Elvis tribute in Tupelo is not at the birthplace. It's not at the Tupelo Museum. The most outstanding Elvis tribute in Tupelo is at the local **McDonald's**.

The Elvis McDonald's, at 372 South Gloster, one block south of Main Street, is not the superficial window-dressing you might expect; it's a comprehensive overview of every aspect of this burg's King. The first indication that this is going to be something special is the depiction of three different eras of Elvis—Hillbilly Cat, Movie Star, Vegas Performer Extraordinaire—etched lovingly into the divider between the counter and the tables.

Offbeat information bites—organized thematically—covering every wall will captivate even the most advanced Elvisologist: the complete TCB oath; quotes aplenty from and about the King; thoughtful insights into various aspects and periods of Elvis's life, including a trenchant look at Colonel Parker's conflict-of-interest arrangement with the Las Vegas Hilton; and a display case with books, trading cards, records, coffee cups, commemorative plates, and more. Sorry, the only thing for sale here is that great McDonald's food.

Open Sunday–Thursday, 6:00 A.M.–11:00 P.M.; Friday and Saturday, 6:00 A.M.–1:00 A.M.

Images of the King surround you at the world's greatest eating establishment devoted to Elvis Presley.

ELVIS BOOKS

The **Cottage Bookshop**, at 214 North Madison Street, specializes in books on Wales, Hunting and Fishing, and Elvis. It's open Monday–Saturday, noon–5:00 P.M. (601) 844-1553.

WHERE TO CAMP

Elvis Presley Lake and Campground is five miles north of the birthplace, east off Canal Extended, north of New Highway 78. Admission to the lake is $1. Campsites range from $5 to $10 a night. For information, call (601) 841-1304.

ROAD TRIPS

Ackerman: Choctaw County, an hour southwest of Tupelo, was home to the Blackwood Brothers, a popular gospel quartet that Elvis admired. After they were discovered, they relocated to Shenandoah, Iowa, then ended up in Memphis. Elvis got to know the group's members there; they sang at Gladys's funeral.

Clarksdale: It was at a crossroads, according to blues lore, that Robert Johnson, the King of Delta Blues Singers, made a pact with the devil and was endowed with genius. Even those who refuse to buy into the myth concede that if there *were* a crossroads, it would be where Highway 61 meets Highway 49 in northwest Mississippi. Although that intersection, in Clarksdale, is not as rustic as it was back around 1930, when Johnson supposedly sealed that Faustian bargain, it is the place to start when looking for the blues.

Clarksdale's fledgling **Delta Blues Museum** features video, audio, and live-music programs as well as memorabilia that includes a photo of Elvis with fellow Memphian B. B. King; a life-size figure of Muddy Waters along with the Muddywood, an electric guitar fashioned from a cypress log salvaged from the cabin in which he was raised; a rusted-out sign from Three Forks, the juke joint where Robert Johnson last played before he was murdered; and a diddley bow (as in Bo Diddley), a one-stringed broom-handle instrument, which visitors may plunk.

There's an annual Delta Blues Festival in early August. Info on the museum and festival: (601) 624-4461.

114 Delta Street. The museum is open Monday–Friday, 9:00 A.M.–5:00 P.M.; Saturday, 10:00 A.M.–2:00 P.M. Admission is by donation.

Jim O'Neal's **Stackhouse** record store, at 232 Sunflower Avenue, features delta music and, like the museum, is a great place to meet an international assortment of enthusiasts and musicians. The store is open Monday–Saturday, noon–6:00 P.M.

Meridan: In May 1953 Elvis competed in the first Jimmie Rodgers Festival; he came in second and won a guitar. He appeared again in May 1955. Rodgers was considered the Father of Country Music; there's a **Jimmie Rodgers Museum** here in Highland Park, open year round. (601) 485-1808.

Morgan City: Robert Johnson, the King of the Delta Blues Singers, was buried here in the **Zion Church graveyard**, off Highway 7. A memorial is at the fund-raising stage.

Ocean Springs: Elvis and his parents took a few summer breathers at the Gulf Hills Dude Ranch during the hysteria of 1956. He swam at the Surf 'n' Sand motel in Biloxi and dated local girl June Juanico. Both properties are gone.

Oxford: The **University of Mississippi Blues Archives** maintains books and files on blues music, but doesn't have any museum-type displays. It's in Room 340 of Farley Hall. Open Monday–Friday, 8:30 A.M.–5:00 P.M. Info: (601) 232-7753.

Mike McGregor Custom Jewelry and Leatherwork offers gaudy "concert belts" like the ones Elvis used to wear, priced from $135 to $310. McGregor used to work the horses, including Elvis's beloved Rising Sun, at Graceland when the King was alive. Route 4, Box 195, Oxford, Mississippi 38655. (601) 234-6970.

3
Memphis

There's no better way to get a sense of what it was like to be Elvis than to trace the circuit of his everyday life in Memphis. Many of his old haunts have been altered or obliterated, but this is not a town that has been developed beyond recognition: a lot of Elvis remains—from his days of poverty to his glory years tooling around on a Harley in the predawn hours to his diverse passions and whimsies of the seventies.

ELVIS SLEPT HERE

The Presleys moved to Memphis from Tupelo in September 1948. A quick review of their living quarters makes it clear that without Elvis's success they would have lived out their lives in a succession of squalid rooms.

When they first arrived in Memphis, the Presleys found a dingy, furnished single room with a communal bathroom on the first floor of a house at 572 Poplar Avenue. It's now an empty lot. They lived here for eight months before scoring a subsidized city apartment.

From May 1949 to January 1953 the Presleys lived in two-bedroom splendor in the red-brick **Lauderdale Courts** housing projects. Here Elvis met Bill Black, who would later become his bassist. (Black lived nearby, at 465 Alabama Street.) The Presleys were evicted when, as Elvis approached high-school graduation and was starting to earn some real money, the family income became too high to qualify for the apartment.

The building is still here, at 185 Winchester Street, just east of Third Avenue. Their first-floor apartment, Number 328, is to the right of the main entrance. It has a fine view of I-40 and, in the distance, the Great American Pyramid!

The Presleys reluctantly moved down in class from Lauderdale Courts to 698 Saffarans, Vernon grumbling that it was impossible for a fellow to get ahead. But a few months later, in April 1953, they found a better place, at 462 Alabama Street, just a few blocks from Lauderdale Courts. It was a duplex; their upstairs neighbor was a rabbi. This is where Elvis was living when he got the first callback from Sam Phillips. It's since been paved over as a ramp for I-40.

By December 1954, thanks to Elvis, things had gotten a little better, so they rented their first real home, a

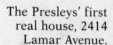

The Presleys' first real house, 2414 Lamar Avenue.

four-room brick ranch in another neighborhood, at **2414 Lamar Avenue**. In 1968 the building became the Tiny Tot nursery school, and later the Cooperative Day Care Center; at last report it was vacant and for sale. The house is on a heavily trafficked strip not far from the airport. There are few neighboring residences. One, across the street, is currently home to Sister Ruby, Fortune Teller.

From the middle of 1955 till May 1956, they lived at **1414 Getwell Road**. A recent owner, upon moving out, tried unsuccessfully to sell bricks from the house to fans for $10 each—the first Elvis abode to be so exploited. He didn't have much luck. What remained of the house was

There goes the neighborhood: hundreds of fans would congregate outside the Presleys' house on Audubon Drive.

eventually moved off the land, and a Chief Auto Parts store now sits on the site.

The first home the family owned was an attractive ranch house at **1034 Audubon Drive**, in a quiet—until Elvis moved in—neighborhood near Memphis State University. After Elvis signed his first movie deal, he plunked down $40,000 for this neat white house; in May 1956 the

Presleys moved in. At this point, Elvis was still accessible to his fans, who would cluster outside the wrought-iron fence waiting for a glimpse. The neighbors apparently were not as horrified as one might expect; their impression of Elvis was generally favorable. But privacy was impossible, and the Presleys moved to Graceland within a year.

Elvis stayed put at Graceland for the next two decades. In the early sixties, he bought a house behind Graceland for Vernon, Dee (Elvis's stepmom), and Dee's three children. The address was **1850 Dolan Road**, but the street has apparently been renumbered—or maybe I just had a brain tumor that day. It's a white split-level, three houses in from the podiatrist on the corner of Elvis Presley Boulevard. Vernon sold it in 1978.

HUMES HIGH

When he arrived in Memphis in 1948, Elvis enrolled at the Christine School, on 3rd Street, to finish eighth grade. He transferred the next year to **L. C. Humes High**, which he attended until his 1953 graduation. Academically, he was a little below average, with a particular weakness in literature but with good marks in phys ed. He had to quit the football team, though, in order to work after school to earn lunch money. (The school mascot is the tiger which coincidentally was Elvis's nom de karate.)

His fellow students included class president George Klein and the muscular Bobby "Red" West, who once stopped a bunch of jocks from beating on Elvis. Both became key members of Graceland's inner circle until their dismissals in the mid-seventies. West also wrote songs and did some Hollywood stunt work, and Klein was a popular Memphis disc jockey.

The school has set aside an Elvis room as both tribute and inspiration. A large golden bust of Elvis was

Golden bust inside the Elvis Room at Humes High. If you study hard, kids, this can be you— not!

presented to Humes on the 10th anniversary of his death; it joins a wall of plaques proclaiming Elvis Presley Day in various states and a bronze copy of his birth certificate.

Under glass is a copy of the priceless 1953 Humes

Humes High, where Elvis slogged through classes.

yearbook, signed by Elvis; the inscription next to his picture says "The King of Hollywood: *You Never Know.*" There's also a 1953 graduation program, copies of Elvis's junior-high and high-school diplomas and ROTC certificate, a rare old photo taken outside Lauderdale Courts, and blown-up high school photos of George Klein and Bobby West. The room is a time capsule as well, displaying typical Humes trophies of 1953 and a vintage classroom and football locker.

The auditorium where Elvis once performed in a talent show is now the Elvis A. Presley Auditorium. No other high school anywhere has gone this all-out for one of its grads: clearly, Elvis is the most prestigious high school alumnus on earth.

When Dewey Phillips, in his first radio interview with Elvis, asked him what high school he attended, it was a subtle way to inform listeners that Elvis was white. Today it would mean just the opposite. Humes is now a junior high, for grades seven through nine. Local teens attend Northside High.

L. C. Humes Junior High. 659 North Manassas Avenue. To visit the Elvis Presley Room, phone ahead to Loretta Griffin at (901) 543-6700, ext. 6695.

ELVIS WORKED HERE

Elvis held several jobs through high school and after graduation.

- He ushered briefly in 1950 at the Loew's State Theater, 152 South Main. He was fired for taking a punch at another usher.
- Elvis worked the late shift at Marl Metal Products, 208 Georgia Avenue, while still in high school, but he got so drowsy in classes that Gladys made him quit.
- He also worked around that time at Upholsteries Specialties Company, 210 West Georgia Avenue.

- Two days after graduating from Humes, Elvis began working at **M. B. Parker Co., Inc.**, 1449 Thomas. He used his first paycheck to realize a lifelong dream—to make a record, which he cut at Sun. After hs brief stint at M. B. Parker, Elvis moved on to Precision Tool factory, 1132 Kansas Street.
- Elvis's best job was driving a truck for Crown Electric Company, where he was working when he got Sam Phillips's call from Sun. (And where, earlier, singer Johnny Burnette was working when he got *his* big break.) He took the job for less money than he was making at Precision Tool because he wanted the freedom of a trucker, and for a while it looked like his destiny. He didn't quit till November 1954, after his smash success on "The Louisiana Hayride."

    Crown was at 353 Poplar Avenue. It had become B & H Hardware, but the owner of B & H pledged that he would close up if he ever got robbed. He did, and was conked on the head to boot; the building was torn down to make way for an Exxon station.

WHERE IT ALL BEGAN

If not for Sam Phillips and his Sun Records label, it's doubtful you'd be reading this wonderful book. In fact, it's possible that you'd be gaining a better understanding of Debby Boone's dad from *Roadside Pat*, that Bruce Springsteen and Jon Bon Jovi would be shoveling toxic waste in central Jersey, and that MTV and Casey Kasem's American Top 40 Countdown would be bringing you the latest in *classical music*!

Whew, what a nightmare. But fortunately, Elvis walked into the **Memphis Recording Service** with four bucks to cut himself a record one day, Sam's assistant

Marion Keisker took note of him, Phillips summoned him months later to try and re-record a "race" record, Elvis got hooked up with Scotty Moore and Bill Black, after several listless tries they began jamming, and Elvis turned out to have an electrifying stage presence.

So "Where It All Began" is really not far from the truth as slogans go. And Sun Studio, which opened for tours and recording in the late eighties after seventeen years of abandonment, is a mandatory stop on the Elvis trail. The studio has been furnished with instruments and equipment from the 1950s as well as photos of the stars who began here, including Jerry Lee Lewis, Johnny Cash, Carl Perkins, Roy Orbison, Charlie Rich, B. B. King, Howlin' Wolf, and a legion of less-celebrated country and rhythm & blues pioneers.

On the tour, you'll hear snatches of Sun recordings, like "Rocket 88"—perhaps the first rock & roll song ever—and a version of "That's When Your Heartaches Begin" played by Elvis, Jerry Lee Lewis, and Carl Perkins in what was known as the million-dollar-quartet session.

Sun Studio, where Elvis cut his first sides and grasped the golden ladder.

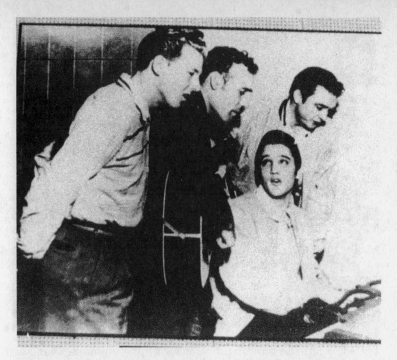

Photo of the Million Dollar Quartet at Sun Studio: Jerry Lee Lewis, Carl Perkins, Elvis, Johnny Cash.

(Johnny Cash, who was billed as the fourth quartet member, had actually left the building before the tape began to roll.) You'll hear the story of Elvis's first session with Scotty and Bill. And you'll hear an *amazing* recording that was long thought nonexistent—disc jockey Dewey Phillips's (no relation to Sam) first spin of Elvis's knockout debut, "That's All Right (Mama)," which Dewey just throws out over the airwaves without pomp or circumstance. This gem, from July 1954, is available on cassette from Sun for $5.

The ceiling, light fixtures, and floor are all original. None of the instruments have any history, however, and only one mike does—it's the one Dewey used for his "Red Hot and Blue" radio show. In recent years, albums have been cut here by U2, Ringo, Dennis Quaid, Jerry Lee

Elvis has left the building, but he's still making money for Sun Studio.

Lewis, and Carl Perkins. You can lay down your own lead vocals over a music track: $49.95 for a half hour. Be the next Elvis! Except you get a cassette, not an acetate.

Souvenirs are big business here: the choice item is a T-shirt or sweatshirt with the Sun logo. Write for a catalog: Sun Studio, 706 Union Street, Memphis, Tennessee 38103.

You can catch the **Sun Shuttle** at Graceland, in front of the Graceland Recording Studio. It includes stops at such Elvis and Memphis sites as Humes High, Beale Street, Lauderdale Courts, and the Elvis statue. 1990 prices were $10 adults, $6 kids, including the studio tour.

Sun Records moved in the late fifties to 639 Madison Avenue, the present-day home of **Sam Phillips Recording Service, Inc.** It's a great-looking building with fifties-style architecture.

Sun Studio, 706 Union Street. Summer hours are 9:00 A.M.–7:00 P.M. daily. Tours every hour on the half hour. (901) 521-0664. The tour costs $4 for adults, $3 kids 4–12.

Taylor's Restaurant, next to Sun Studio, was a popular hangout for Sun artists. It's now the fifties-ish **Sun Studio Cafe**, serving burgers, barbecue, and peanut-butter-and-banana sandwiches. You can buy Sun souvenirs here, too. 710 Union Avenue, at Marshall Street. Open 9:00 A.M.–9:00 P.M. daily.

Dewey Phillips's "Red Hot and Blue" show was broadcast from the mezzanine of the Chiska (Chickasaw) Hotel, 272 South Main Street, at Linden Avenue. The original building still stands, but it's now the Church of

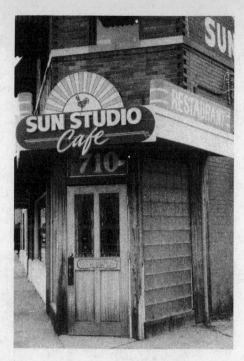

Sun Studio Cafe,
formerly Taylor's,
an Elvis hangout.

God in Christ. (Their motto: "Jesus Saves.") Dewey's radio
station, WHBQ, was bought by Sam Phillips and renamed WLVS.

Bob Neal, another disc jockey of importance to Elvis,
broadcast his show on WMPS, 112 Union, across the
street from Memphis's most famous hotel, the **Peabody**.
Neal became Elvis's first real manager when Scotty, who
had been handling the chores, became overwhelmed.
Neal's management company, Memphis Promotions, was
based at 160 Union Avenue; he also had a record store on
Main Street, next to the Warner Theater. Neal helped
finance Elvis's first Caddy. He was squeezed out when
the Colonel caught wind of Elvis.

Elvis bought his R&B platters in the early fifties at
Home of the Blues, a record store at Beale and Main
Streets. The site is now a parking lot. He also bought
records through the years at **Poplar Tunes**, which was

A photo of Elvis with Dewey Phillips and Joe Coughi dominates the wall at Poplar Tunes.

owned by Joe Coughi, who later formed Hi Records. It's still there, at 308 Poplar Avenue, near Lauderdale Courts. There's a very, very large photo of Elvis with Joe and Dewey Phillips on the wall.

Elvis's first publicity photos were shot at **Blue Light Studios**, which was formerly at Beale and 2nd and is now at 145 South Main Street, on the depressing Mid-America Mall.

ELVIS SANG HERE

Over the years, lots of club owners claimed that Elvis sang at their joints while in high school, or earlier. More than likely, those guys were just trying to grab some cheap attention.

Elvis did perform at the Bon Air Club in July 1954 with Doug Poindexter and his Starlight Wranglers, for whom Scotty Moore played guitar. It was his first appearance after the release of "That's All Right (Mama)." The club was at 4862 Summer Avenue, at Mendenhall Road, but it's now gone.

The Bon Air Club is not to be confused with the Bel Air Club, 1850 South Bellevue Boulevard, where Elvis also appeared early on. The ramshackle **Motel Bel-Air** is still here, offering convenient hourly rates.

The most significant early Elvis club dates were at Sleepy-Eyed John's Eagle's Nest, a now-defunct ballroom on Highway 78 at Clearpool and Lamar Avenues. It's the first place he sang solo, and he appeared here many times. Supposedly, Oscar "The Baron" Davis, who had been Hank Williams's manager and was then scouting for Colonel Parker, saw him here and alerted the Colonel. Elvis also rocked the Airport Inn in 1955; it, too, is gone.

Elvis's first gig after bombing on the Opry in September 1954 was singing with Scotty and Bill from a flatbed truck at the opening of the Katz Drug Store, in the Lamar-Airways Shopping Center, 2256 Lamar Avenue; the building is now an American Thrift store.

Elvis made his first big splash singing and gyrating as an opener for Slim Whitman on July 30, 1954, at the **Overton Park Shell**. He was billed as Ellis Presley. At an August 1955 concert here he upstaged Webb Pierce, who allegedly hissed, "Sonuvabitch!"—"in jest." Overton Park can be entered at the corner of North Parkway and East Parkway.

At **Ellis Auditorium** in February 1961, the King made his first post-army appearance—it was his next-to-last live concert for eight years. He also attended gospel shows here as early as 1952; he saw the Blackwood Brothers and learned to play piano here. It's also said that James Blackwood used to sneak him in for free. It's still there, on Main Street and Exchange, a confusing architectural stew dwarfed by the new megaprojects nearby.

In 1969, for the first time in 14 years, Elvis recorded in Memphis. He cut *From Elvis in Memphis* and half of *From Memphis to Vegas/From Vegas to Memphis* at Chips Moman's American Sound Studios. The studio, at 827 Danny Thomas Street, is now a Chief Auto Parts store, but fortunately Jimmy Velvet salvaged key objects for his Elvis museums.

Elvis recorded some songs in 1973 for the *Promised Land, Good Times*, and *Raised on Rock/For Ol' Times Sake* LPs at the **Stax recording studio**, the one-time Olympus of soul music, where Sam and Dave, Wilson Pickett (that's *Pickett* . . . not those three goony girls), the Staple Singers, Eddie Floyd, and Booker T and the MGs cut some of their best sides. The studio at 625 East McLemore Avenue, east of Parkway Avenue, was demolished in 1991. (The **Rum Boogie Cafe**, 182 Beale, has the original neon Stax sign.)

The **Mid-South Coliseum** was almost named after Elvis in 1971, but the city council gave him Highway 51 (South Bellevue Boulevard) instead. In 1974 he recorded a concert album here. He was booked to perform at the Coliseum a few days after he died. It's in the fairgrounds, next to Libertyland, northeast of the intersection of Southern Avenue and East Parkway.

ELVIS'S WOMEN

Elvis's senior prom was held at the Peabody; his date was Regis Wilson. Even as an awkward high schooler, he didn't have a lot of trouble getting dates. The next year he escorted Dixie Locke, his first serious girlfriend, to her senior prom.

After Elvis managed to coax 17-year-old Priscilla's father into letting her stay at Graceland (with Vernon and Dee as "chaperones"), he had Vernon enroll her at **Immaculate Conception High**, a tony parochial school where students wear plaid skirts; she graduated June 1964. It's on Central Avenue and Belvedere Boulevard.

Priscilla was also sent to the Patricia Stevens Finishing School (on Madison Avenue) to study dance and modeling, and to the Jo Haynes School of Dancing (4769 Elvis Presley Boulevard) to study ballet. Both are now defunct.

Priscilla would model under an alias in after-school fashion shows at the **Piccadilly Cafeteria**, 3968 Elvis Presley Boulevard, in Whitehaven Plaza—she needed the spending money. But Elvis wanted her available at his whim, so he forced her to quit.

Elvis bought a house for Ginger Alden, his last girlfriend and possible fiancée, at **4152 Royal Crest Place**,

Priscilla modeled fashions at this cafeteria after school: "Pass the compote—hey, nice dress."

on the extreme eastern side of town. After Elvis died, Ginger's mother sued the estate for $40,000, claiming he had promised to pay off her mortgage; she lost.

ELVIS IN THE WHEEEE! HOURS

ROWDY FUN

In his younger days, Elvis would rent the Fairgrounds Amusement Park after-hours for himself and his friends at $2,500 per night. He especially liked the bumper cars. The park is now called **Libertyland**, and it's in the fairgrounds, off Eastern Parkway, between Central and Southern Avenues. Libertyland generally schedules something, like an Elvis impersonator, during International Tribute Week. Call (901) 274-1776 for hours and prices.

Elvis also rented out the Rainbow Rollerdome for private parties that were more like war on wheels; he held a veritable eight-night roller-skating orgy just before his induction into the army. It was at 2881 Lamar Avenue, but it's gone.

MR. MOVIES

On the July 1954 night "That's All Right (Mama)" was to receive its first on-air spin, Elvis was bashfully hiding out at Suzore's No. 2 Movie Theater. Elvis would take dates to this second-run theater, then go to Charlie's snack and record emporium across the street to listen to rhythm & blues. Suzore's was at 279 North Main Street; both were demolished years ago.

Later on, Elvis would rent out the Memphian Theatre for private after-hour screenings; he would watch old favorites, new releases, and movies starring actresses he had dated. He met Linda Thompson here in the early seventies. The Memphian, now the lavender **Playhouse Theater**, is at 51 South Cooper, near Madison.

The Orpheum, formerly the Malco, which Elvis would rent for private screenings.

Another theater he would rent, the Malco, is now the **Orpheum**; this restored palace, with a beautiful marquee, hosts ballet, theater, opera, concerts, and special events. Main and Beale Streets. Info: (901) 525-3000.

Some other theaters, all now defunct, that he would rent were the Crosstown, 400 North Cleveland; the Avon, at 124 West Broadway, in West Memphis, Arkansas; and the Ridgeway, which Elvis had booked for a screening of *MacArthur* on the last day of his life—it had to be canceled because they couldn't find a projectionist.

RESTAURANTS AND CLUBS

Sadly, most places where Elvis hung out have bitten the dust. These include the Coffee Cup diner, in West Memphis, Arkansas, where he and his fellow recruits stopped for a bite on the way to Fort Chaffee in 1958. In the sixties, Elvis and his pals hung out in the Delta Room at Chenault's restaurant, 1400 Elvis Presley Boulevard, between Quinn and Gill. It's since been remodeled and reopened as G.J.'s Family Restaurant, with no traces of Elvis.

Elvis and Priscilla would generally rent out a club each New Year's Eve for a party; unfortunately, none of them remain. They celebrated in 1962 (17-year-old Priscilla got thoroughly plastered), 1963, 1965, and 1966 at the Manhattan Club, on Bellevue Boulevard. In 1966 word leaked out to the public about the party; when Elvis pulled up and saw the crowds, he turned around and went home. They held the 1968 New Year's Eve party at the Thunderbird Lounge. Elvis would also rent out T.J.'s nightclub, which was managed by one of the Guys, Alan Fortas.

Elvis would load up on burgers (well-done) at the **Gridiron Restaurant**, 4101 Elvis Presley Boulevard. It's still there, less than a mile from Graceland.

Two restaurants where Elvis never chowed down offer an Elvis experience nonetheless. The walls of **Broadway Pizza**, at 2581 Broad Avenue, boast framed locks of Elvis's hair, his karate black belt, and paintings,

Where Elvis would buy cheeseburgers.

drawings, busts, and posters of the King. The photos were brought in by a customer named Alan—he turned out to be Alan Fortas. George Klein also stops in on occasion. Dewana Anne Plaunk, the daughter of the owners, Douglas and Janet Cox, is a beauty queen and karate star; her memorabilia is here, too. Like Elvis, she studied karate with Kang Rhee. And the **Pizza Hut** at 4290 Elvis Presley Boulevard has an Elvis Presley Room, with a wall-size mural, nine portraits, and an Elvis-stocked juke box.

ELVIS SHOPPED HERE

CAR CRAZY

Elvis was the best private customer the auto industry has ever known. He would buy fleets of luxury cars for himself, his friends, casual acquaintances, and perfect strangers.

The dudes who customized Elvis's bikes and trikes.

At Southern Motors, later called Madison Cadillac, Elvis bought 14 Eldorados one July day in 1975. It was at 341 Union Avenue, but business tailed off after Elvis died, and it's gone. Robertson Motors, now **Autorama**, is where Elvis bought many Mercedeses. It's at 2950 Airways Boulevard, near the airport. One day in 1974, Elvis bought out the stock of five Lincoln Continental Mark IVs at **Schilling Lincoln-Mercury**, 987 Union Avenue. The place is thriving to this day.

Elvis had his trikes and Harleys and Lisa Marie's golf cart customized by Lew Elliott, co-owner of **Supercycle**. Elliott had sold Elvis and Priscilla their black hair dye in his earlier days as a Clairol distributor. There are extensive clips and photos here of Elvis and his bikes, but the highlight is a replica of the supertrike that was built for Elvis in 1975 and is now on display at the Automobile Museum at Graceland. Supercycle will gladly produce another replica for any cash-heavy Elvis fan that wants one.

Supercycle also restored Elvis's snowmobiles, pink jeep, and 1966 HD chopper—Elvis and the Guys were notorious for trashing their toys. You can buy a poster of Elvis astride a Harley for $9.95.

624 South Bellevue Boulevard. (901) 725-5991.

CLOTHES HORSE
Lansky's Clothing Emporium, known as Lansky Brothers, catered to fashion-conscious Memphis blacks in the fifties; Elvis would window-shop as a teen, then bought most of his wardrobe here after hitting it big. In 1957 Elvis swapped owner Bernard Lansky a three-wheeled Messerschmidt for free run of the store; Lansky still has the car.

Lansky's became Hercules Budget Stores for the Big and Tall Man, but that closed in the late eighties. The Lansky's sign remains on the side of the building, as well as the slogan "Clothier to the King"; a musical mural

Lansky's, Clothier to the King.

along the western wall includes a depiction of Elvis, natch.

Bernard Lansky reopened the site as a gift shop, open only the week of the birthday celebration and in the summer. You can get Lansky's T-shirts as well as the standard Graceland stuff here. Some photos are here, but not the secret hidden ones that Lansky plans to exhibit some day.

Lansky wants to set up a full-blown museum called Lansky's Elvis Presley Museum that will display "unpublished photos," the Messerschmidt, and something familiar to those who have visited Lansky's in the past—"Elvis's dressing mirror." Of course, there will also be lots of clothes. "I put Elvis in his first suit and his last suit," Lansky claims. "And I dressed him for 'The Ed Sullivan Show.'" If you visit his store, Lansky will gleefully regale you with captivating Elvis clothing stories.

126 Beale Street, at 2nd Avenue, across from the Elvis statue. (901) 525-1521.

Elvis bought flowers here. You can, too.

FLOWERS AND DIAMONDS

Elvis patronized **Burke's Florist**, 1609 Elvis Presley Boulevard, just north of Forest Hills Cemetery. Burke's has set up window displays during International Tribute Week.

Elvis bought lots of diamonds and rings—including Priscilla's wedding ring—from Harry Levitch of Harry Levitch Jewelers, 159 Union Avenue. It's gone.

Lowell G. Hays & Sons was Elvis's favorite diamond dealer; they designed the TCB ring and Maltese cross. Today, they'll sell you a TCB or TLC necklace: the price fluctuates, but it's usually between $480 and $600. There's a painting of Elvis in an inner office. 4872 Poplar Avenue. (901) 767-2840.

HOME IMPROVEMENT

Charles Church, who ran a shop called Law Enforcement, sold Elvis many guns and designed the Graceland security system. There's now a Law Enforcement Electronics in town, but it's not the same one.

Bill Eubanks, of **McCormick-Eubanks Interior Design**, helped redecorate Graceland in 1974 when Linda Thompson moved in. The shop, at 1793 Union Avenue, looks like a precious little cottage.

Doors, Inc., created the Graceland "music gates" in 1957 and refurbished them in 1990. It's at 911 Rayner Street, in an industrial part of town.

Elvis piled up the black belts at Kang Rhee.

KARATE

One day in 1969, Kang Rhee, proprietor of the **Kang Rhee Institute of Self-Defense**, got a call from someone claiming to be Elvis; he assumed it was a prankster. Elvis showed up an hour later, however; he soon became a prized friend and pupil, earning advanced black belts. Rhee traveled to Vegas with Elvis and gave self-defense seminars to the TCB gang. Elvis had a Vegas costume-maker do his first ghi; he had it made tight, like his jumpsuits. The first time Elvis did a kick in it, the crotch ripped open—and Elvis wasn't wearing any underwear.

Tours of the institute have been given during Tribute Week, with Rhee signing autographs and talking about Elvis. He displays an autographed guitar, jewelry, his lifetime backstage pass, and photos of Elvis in karate action, all given to him by his pal, the King. Rhee is happy to show these to fans who drop by. You can even have your photo taken holding the guitar.

After many years at 1911 Poplar Avenue, Rhee moved the school in 1990 to 706 Germantown Parkway, #70, in the Trinity Commons Shopping Center, in Cordova, east of town. Phone: (901) 757-5000.

Elvis gave a karate demonstration in 1974 at the Tennessee Karate Institute, which was owned at the time by Red West. It was at 1372 Overton, above a drugstore, but it's gone.

CIVIC MATTERS

The Memphis Draft Board, Local 86, that notified Elvis on December 19, 1957, that the army wanted him was at 198 South Main Street, Room 215. Among the officers who processed him was Walter Alden, the father of an infant, Ginger, who in two decades would become Elvis's best girl. Elvis was actually inducted March 24, 1958, after receiving a 60-day deferment to complete *King Creole*. The office is now called the Military Entrance Processing Station and is located at 161 Jefferson.

The local government wasn't through with Elvis after his death. Colonel Parker tangled with the executors of Elvis's estate in **Memphis Probate Court**, 140 Adams Avenue. Parker lost. And in the **City Council Chamber**, at City Hall (Front Street at Adams), Dr. Nick's Board of Medical Examiners hearing took place; city law required public proceedings, and there was a big turnout. Although he faced more serious charges—Geraldo says he *killed Elvis*, for gosh sakes—Dr. Nick was nailed only for faulty record keeping and was suspended for three months.

HOSPITALS

Several Memphis hospitals have an Elvis connection, and not all of the associations are unpleasant. Elvis's spirit of charity, and the charity of his fans after his death, have left their mark.

- The saddest chamber in Elvis's life was Room 688 of **Methodist Hospital** (1265 Union Avenue), where his mom died on August 14, 1958.

- **St. Jude's Children's Research Hospital** (264 Jackson Avenue), founded by Danny Thomas, is where Elvis met Patsy Cline, the Queen of Country Music. Elvis later made a unique donation to the hospital: after buying Franklin D. Roosevelt's yacht, the *Potomac*, he turned around and presented it to St. Jude's for auction.

- **Baptist Memorial Hospital**, 899 Madison Avenue, is a veritable rock quarry of *Roadside Elvis* milestones. Of course, this is where Elvis was pronounced dead (in Trauma Room 1) and later autopsied, but he also checked in various times in the 1970s: in October 1973, he had a room on the 16th floor; in January 1975 he was put on the 18th floor; and in April 1977 he took a two-room suite on the 16th floor. Elvis took a shine to his nurse, Mrs. Marion Cocke, author of *I Called Him Babe*, during his 1975 stay.

  Lisa Marie was born here February 1, 1968.

Vernon convalesced here after his first heart attack, and Bill Black died here of a heart attack in 1965.

Many of Dr. Nick's scripts were filled at **The Prescription House**. Pharmacist Jack Kirsch, who provided 5,684 pills for Elvis, lost his license for life in 1980. The pharmacy was a few blocks from Baptist Hospital, at 1247 Madison Avenue; it's now at 1800 Union Avenue. There is no Elvis display.

- **The Elvis Presley Memorial Trauma Center**, the only institution in the world officially named after Elvis and the third-busiest trauma center in the U.S.A., has a Wall of Honor of plaques thanking fans and clubs who donate $1,000 or more. Tours have been given during Tribute Week. To contribute, write to the attention of Marler Stone at 877 Jefferson Avenue, Memphis, Tennessee 38103, or call Stone at the Med, (901) 575-8372. Make checks payable to the Medical Foundation.

- **Le Bonheur Children's Medical Center**, Adams Street at Dunlap, also has an Elvis Presley Wall with names of $1,000 donators. The Burning Love Fan Club, of Streamwood, Illinois, has bought 23 of the 60 or so total plaques here. Info: (901) 522-3030.

DEATH, BE NOT CRUEL

It's no fun talking about anything concerning Elvis's death, so let's get through this quickly.

- The paramedics called in to revive Elvis when he

was found slumped in the bathroom were summoned from the Memphis Fire Department, **Engine House No. 29**, 2147 Elvis Presley Boulevard.

- The bodies of Elvis, Gladys, Vernon, and Bill Black were all prepared for burial at the **Memphis Funeral Home**, 1177 Union Avenue. Services for Gladys were held here; 700 people showed up, and the Blackwood Brothers sang. The home is a handsome white Prairie-style building with green-tinted windows the color of sunglass lenses.

The bodies of Elvis, Gladys, and Vernon were all prepared for burial at the Memphis Funeral Home.

- Gladys and Elvis were initially interred in a mausoleum at **Forest Hill Cemetery**. Shortly after Elvis's burial, three men were accused of trying to steal his body; it's not at all clear what really happened, but the result was that both were reburied in the Meditation Garden at Graceland. Uncle Travis Smith—Gladys's brother, who was stationed at the Graceland gates for years—and his wife, Loraine, are buried here. 1661 Elvis Presley Boulevard, three miles north of Graceland.

- In 1978 Bill Carwile of **Carwile's Dry Cleaners** bought the original Forest Hills tombs of Elvis and Gladys. He chopped Elvis's marble slab into 44,000 two-inch-by-one-inch chunks and tried to sell them for $89.95 each—there were few takers. He cut the price to $39.95 but still only unloaded a dozen or so. Carwile learned the hard way about Elvis fans and death. He also bought the entrance gate to the mausoleum—that's lying around somewhere, too. He lost a bundle, but he seems to have a cheerful attitude about it.

  A brochure enclosed with each chunk of marble reveals that it was removed under "stringent security," measured and recorded by a notary public, then stored in a double-alarm-system security vault. Give Carwile some credit for trying; his business is at 2178 Central Avenue.

BEALE STREET

Beale Street was the throbbing heart of the Memphis R&B scene in the old days; Elvis hung out here after work in the mid-fifties. Although cute-ized, it's still the place to go in town for music. But first, check out the **Elvis statue** on Beale, in Elvis Presley Plaza. This civic tribute was unveiled in August 1980. Next, look for Elvis's brass musical note on the **Walk of Fame**, along with notes for B. B. King, Isaac Hayes, Alberta Hunter, and other Memphis heavies. For Beale Street info, call (901) 526-0110.

Alfred's, at 197 Beale, has an entire room devoted to the King. Here you'll find copies of his gold records, a big model of Graceland with the Hillbilly Cat out front saying howdy, a certified pair of Elvis's white socks, a

Memphis's civic tribute to America's favorite son.

Nipper, Elvis's "favorite" leather jacket (with red fur trim), a Hilton-logo scarf from his Vegas days, and more. George Klein plays here at times with his Rock & Roll Revue.

The **Memphis Police Museum** has an Elvis tribute case, including an official memo informing fellow officers of the death of Staff Reserve Officer Elvis Presley, the honorary Captain of the Memphis Police Reserve Program. There's also a photo of Elvis with some of the Memphis police. His application (February 9, 1976) for the reserve force is here. On it, he is asked, "Do you own your own car?" His answer: "Yes."

159 Beale Street. The museum, open 24 hours (it's within an actual precinct, right in the heart of the swinging Beale strip), is free.

Finally, **A. Schwab's Dry Goods**, which dates back to 1876 and looks it, offers Elvis souvenirs at lower prices than you'll find at Graceland. Plus, they brag they have men's pants to size 74 and women's dresses to size 60. 163 Beale Street. Open Monday–Saturday, 9:00 A.M.–5:00 P.M.

WHERE TO STAY

- Although the idea of a Graceland Travel Park was scrapped, RVers can camp next to the **Wilson World Hotel**, right across from Graceland. Wilson World, just north of the *Lisa Marie*, is my personal hotel recommendation. It offers free, in-room Elvis movies and Elvis paintings in the lobby, and it's run by Memphian Kemmons Wilson, the founder of Holiday Inn—one channel on the TV constantly shows "The Kemmons Wilson Story." 3677 Elvis Presley Boulevard. Res.: (800) 333-WILSON or (901) 372-0000.

- The Memory Lane Inn, not quite as nice as Wilson World, is the most Elvis-themed motel anywhere. There's an Elvis gift shop in the lobby and free in-room Elvis movies. It, too, is right across the street from Graceland. 3839 Elvis Presley Boulevard. Res.: (800) 874-7084 or (901) 346-5500.

- The Days Inn at 1533 East Brooks Road is where the ever-popular Elvis Window Decorating Contest is held every Tribute Week. It's coordinated by Ms. Pat Thompson. Res.: (901) 345-2470.

- The Memphis Hilton calls itself the "official hotel for Elvis International Tribute Week." 2240 Democrat Road, at Airways. Res.: (800) HILTONS.

- The Peabody Hotel: if you've got the bucks, they've got the ducks. The Peabody, which first opened in 1869 and was rebuilt in 1925, is world-renowned for its March of the Ducks: every morning at eleven they stride down to the lobby; every afternoon at five they return to their nest on the roof. 149 Union Street. Res.: (901) 529-4000.

SIDE TRIPS

Reverend Al Green's Church: The Full Gospel Tabernacle is presided over by one of the sweetest soul and gospel singers of our times—the Reverend Al Green. The public is heartily welcomed to Sunday services: gospel lovers and Green devotees from all over the world have made pilgrimages here. The chances of catching Green on any given Sunday are "about 99 percent," according to a spokesperson, but it wouldn't hurt to call ahead.

787 Hale Road, off Elvis Presley Boulevard, between Raines and Shelby. Every Sunday at 11:00 A.M., plus a sunset service at 5:00 P.M. in the winter, 7:00 P.M. in summer. (901) 396-9192.

The Pyramid: The $72 million (and rising) **Great American Pyramid** was nearing completion at this writing. It's a 321-foot-tall, stainless-steel replica of Egypt's Great Pyramid, with a 20,000-seat arena, Dick Clark's American Music Awards Hall of Fame (oboy), a Hard Rock Cafe, and a museum of American music. Radio station WHBQ is currently broadcasting from the Pyramid's pointy top. There have also been promises of something called the Memphis Musical Experience, which would undoubtedly include some tribute to Elvis. Plans will surely change when it comes time to put up or shut up.

There will also be a walkway of commemorative bricks. You can buy one in a section set aside for Elvis fans and inscribe it with your personal message. The $50 cost is tax deductible. Write to MIFA/Pyramid Bricks, P.O. Box 3311, Memphis, Tennessee 38173, or call: (901) 5-BRICKS [(901) 527-4257].

At Wolf River Harbor and the Mississippi River. Take the Front Street exit off I-40 or the Downtown Memphis exit off I-55. (901) 576-7241 or (800) 62-PYRAMID.

REMEMBER TO FORGET THESE

The following Elvis sites are either long gone or not someplace you'd want to visit. I include them in the name of trivia.

GONE OR MOVED

- Vernon packed crates at the United Paint Company for 83 cents an hour on and off from 1949 till Elvis became famous. United Paint was at 446 Concord Avenue at the time but has since moved to 404 Mallory Avenue.

- WDIA was an influential black station in Elvis's youth; its disc jockeys included B. B. King and Rufus Thomas. The station was at 2074 Union Avenue at the time; it's now at 112 Union Avenue—and 1070 on your AM dial.

- The Plastic Products company, at 1746 Chelsea Avenue, pressed "That's All Right (Mama)"/"Blue Moon of Kentucky" for Sam Phillips in July 1954. It's all gone, mama.

- The Tennessee Employment Security office, where Elvis went in June 1953 for a General Aptitude Test Battery and was sent to a job at M. B. Parker Co., Inc., was at 122 Union Avenue. The building now houses the National Bank of Commerce.
- Dentist Lester Hoffman treated Elvis on the night of August 15, 1977, in his office at 920 Estate. Hoffman no longer is listed in Memphis.

DON'T BOTHER

- The Presley family's First Assembly of God church shifted locations a few times, from 960 South Third Street to 1085 McLemore Street, and finally to 255 Highland Street. Elvis's 1949 Sunday schoolmates included three of the Blackwood Brothers and members of the Stamps, and Assembly Church reverend James E. Hamill eulogized Gladys in 1958. But remember, once he became famous, Elvis couldn't go to such a public place.
- Dr. Nick's office was at 1734 Madison Avenue. His current office is at 6027 Walnut Grove Road.
- Dr. David Meyer, Elvis's eye doctor, now has an office at 825 Ridge Lake Boulevard.
- You can hardly see the "Blvd." in the sign for The Elvis Presley Blvd. Inn and Lounge, 2300 Elvis Presley Boulevard, so you might think it has some kind of Elvis theme. It doesn't. Graceland cannot touch this place because it's technically OK, and besides, it's been around "forever."

ROAD TRIPS

Adamsville: The **Buford Pusser Home & Museum** has the *Walking Tall* sheriff's actual furnishings and memorabilia. Elvis sent Pusser, whom he admired, a large check when his home was burned. Buford and his wife Pauline are buried in the town cemetery, on the west side of town. There's a plaque on Highway 64, five miles west of town, at the site of his fatal car wreck. 342 Pusser Street. (901) 632-4080.

Gadsden: Scotty Moore, Elvis's first guitarist and manager, was born Winfield Scott Moore III here on December 27, 1931. He was living on Belz Street in Memphis when he first met Elvis.

Walls, Mississippi: Elvis's 163-acre **Circle G Ranch** was named after either Graceland or Gladys, but he had to rename it the Flying Circle G after a Circle G ranch in Texas squawked.

Elvis was cruising northern Mississippi in March 1967 with Jerry Schilling and Alan Fortas shopping for horses (he and Priscilla were heavily into riding at the time) when he saw an immense cross in a ranch pasture. He told Fortas to go see if the ranch was for sale. It was; Elvis paid Jack Adams $437,000 for the place, including fixtures.

Elvis bought Rancheros for all the Guys and installed mobile homes for them and their families on the property. He stocked the ranch with two dozen horses and nine to twelve ranch hands. Thanks to the Circle G, the highest-paid star in Hollywood was starting to run out of money.

Elvis and Priscilla spent a week here after their wedding, living in a trailer instead of in the main house; they had gone to the Bahamas for a honeymoon but didn't like it. It's said that Elvis lost his wedding ring somewhere on the grounds—bring your metal detector!

The ranch motif of pink brick is seen in the main house, surrounding wall, and gate house. There's a fireplace at the south end of the ranch enscripted "EP." The cross is still there, but is now hidden behind trees. It could also use a paint job.

The ranch was sold to a gun club, but the club couldn't get a shooting permit, so Elvis bought it back; he unloaded it for good in 1973. After Elvis's death, owner P. Montesi, Jr., started charging fans $2 admission. There were rumors that a later owner wanted to open an Elvis-themed resort, but he gave up. It's now owned by the McLemores, who turned it into the Ranch House restaurant, specializing in catfish (which Elvis hated, by the way). There are some Elvis photos in the restaurant, but the connection is basically unexploited. Too bad.

To get to the Ranch House restaurant from Graceland, go ten miles south—just past the state line—on Elvis Presley Boulevard (Highway 51), then four miles west on Highway 302 (Goodman Road). At the junction of Highway 301 (there's a stop sign) turn left (south) and go a few hundred feet; it's on the east side of the road. Open Wednesday–Sunday, 5:00 P.M.–10:00 P.M. (601) 781-1411.

At last report, the Ranch House was rumored to be on the verge of closing, so definitely call ahead if you plan to visit.

West Memphis, Arkansas: Elvis's Aunt Nash, Vernon's sister, lived here in the 1980s at 702 Dover Road.

4
Graceland

3764 ELVIS PRESLEY BOULEVARD

Is this a holy shrine or what? Just ask Jerry Lee Lewis and Bruce Springsteen. Each sat atop the world of rock & roll in his day, and each was nabbed trying to vault the fence here.

Elvis bought Graceland, a 1939 Southern Colonial minimansion in the south Memphis suburb of White-haven, in March 1957 for a hundred-thousand bucks. It was built by Dr. and Mrs. Thomas Moore; Mrs. Moore's family had been on the land for generations. The house is named after Mrs. Moore's great-aunt Grace.

Graceland sits on a hillock amid a congested patch of Elvis Presley Boulevard, the 12-mile stretch of U.S. 51 that was renamed in Elvis's honor in 1972. When Elvis first moved here, the area was far more pastoral than it is today.

Although hundreds of fans have congregated at the music gate every day before and after Elvis's death, the house was not opened to the public until June 7, 1982, when Priscilla decided that fans should be allowed in, for a price. Since then, Graceland has become one of America's most popular show homes, rivaling the White House, which probably receives more visitors (only because it gives tours for free). Graceland garners 600,000 admissions annually—between 2,500 and 5,000 per day in the summer.

Lisa Marie gets the house in 1993, when she turns 25, but has agreed to leave it open to the public until at least May 1, 1998. Elvis's Aunt Delta, Vernon's sister, still lives in Graceland, in what used to be Vernon and Gladys's room.

Park on the west side of Elvis Presley Boulevard, across the street from the house. After purchasing your tour ticket—there are many options, explained later on—you take a shuttle bus across the boulevard to Graceland. All the other attractions are back on the west side of the street. The Graceland management continually adds new temptations, figuring that many fans are coming again and again, but the tour of the house will always be the heart and soul of the Graceland Experience.

GRACELAND: THE HOUSE

The tour begins in the dining room, where dinner was generally served around 9:00 P.M. or 10:00 P.M. The flashy decor here and in the living room reflects the last refurbishing of the mansion, accomplished under the stewardship of Priscilla in 1982. The house's abundant mirrors, which provide the illusion of space, seem to be the only remaining evidence of Linda Thompson's decorating mastery at Graceland.

The living room features a 15-foot, one-piece couch and a 10-foot coffee table, both custom-made. The piano in the music room was originally white; Priscilla had it wrapped with gold leaf to surprise Elvis.

Since the upstairs is off-limits even to employees, who claim never to have set foot there, the next stop is

The TV room.

downstairs, in the yellow and black TV room, where you
see Elvis's soda fountain and three side-by-side TV sets.
(Altogether, the mansion has 14 TVs.) Elvis got the idea
from LBJ, who would watch three news broadcasts at
once; Elvis, the tour guide points out, was more inter-
ested in sports. The TCB lightning-bolt logo covers one
wall.

Rather than take you all through the mansion, your
guide turns you over to another—you get a different es-
cort in almost every room. Next is the pool room; a tear
in the table's green felt remains unrepaired, but there
really isn't a very good story to explain this. Before moving on, remember: no one is hustling you through—you
can take your time, savor each room, maybe hear the
guide describe it several times.

Next is the wild, wild Jungle Room, the den where
Elvis recorded parts of *Moody Blue* (his last album) and
From Elvis Presley Boulevard, Memphis, Tennessee. The
decor is totally Elvis—a grown-up kid with lots of money
and outlandish tastes: wooden chairs carved in the shape

The pool room.

The Jungle Room, with the most notorious decor in America.

of monkeys, fur-covered lampshades, and green shag carpeting on the ceiling (for acoustics).

Step outside and cross over to Vernon's office, a converted outbuilding. Here you'll see a videotape of a truly funny Elvis fielding questions at a post-army press conference held right here in this room. Vernon, a tightfisted and crude executive, posted a sign on the door aimed at delivery people and other would-be malingerers; it still remains:

> PLEASE READ AND OBSERVE
> NO LOAFING IN OFFICE
> STRICTLY FOR EMPLOYEES ONLY!
> IF YOU HAVE BUSINESS HERE,
> PLEASE TAKE CARE OF IT AND LEAVE
>   VERNON PRESLEY

On to the shooting room, adjoining the office. Here is a display of bullets and casings swept from the floor and pried from the walls. Boy, were the secretaries in Vernon's office surprised the first time the Guys started discharging their weapons just a few feet away!

Stroll back now across the yard to the Trophy Room, which begins with a time line tracing Elvis's life. A dummy is dressed in Elvis's army fatigues. On display is a pair of Elvis's two-toned shoes, his 1956 and 1960 Gibson J-200 guitars (seen in many films), and a TV set given to him by RCA for selling 50 million records.

Elvis's gold records are displayed in the awesome Hall of Gold. When the flash-in-the-pan Limey rock star Boy George visited, he was all wisecracks and attitude until he saw the Hall of Gold—suddenly, his piddly achievements didn't seem so "fab." Also here are Elvis's three Grammys, all for gospel recordings.

A glass case contains a pile of movie scripts. There are movie posters, pictures, his *Kid Galahad* robe, and the double-neck guitar from *Spinout*. A collection of tributes includes honorary police badges, keys to cities, and the DEA badge Elvis snagged from Nixon.

Dummies wear Elvis's wedding tux and Priscilla's wedding dress. (You won't find much post-Priscilla memorabilia here. Remember who controls the estate.) Here also is the black leather ensemble and maroon jacket

The Trophy Room

The costume display at Graceland. Too bad he died when everybody wore such stupid clothes.

from the 1968 Singer special. Elvis's gaudy seventies costumes abound, including the awesome Tiger outfit. Seeing all these clothes together makes you realize what a shame it is that Elvis had to die in the seventies; it makes it look like he had bad taste—but in fact, we all dressed like goons then.

From here you slip back across the yard to the racquetball court, in an outbuilding that was added in 1975 during Elvis's racquetball frenzy. After the bombardment of the Trophy Room, fans are kind of unimpressed here. Especially since the next and last stop is . . .

The Meditation Garden, where Elvis, Vernon, Gladys, and Grandma Minnie Mae (Dodger) are buried. There's also a small memorial to Elvis's twin, Jessie, spelled here with an *i*. You can stay as long as you like, maybe even—I don't know—meditate or something.

After your visit to Meditation Garden you'll wind back down the drive and out into the cold commercial world. On your way, you'll pass Elvis's guitar-shaped swimming pool. Before you dig into those pockets, though, take note that there's a *clearly marked* sign for-

The Meditation Garden at Graceland, where visitors can meditate on how much they will spend on souvenirs across the street.

bidding you to toss coins into the water. Try to remember that it's a pool, not a wishing well, and try to ignore the $2.34 or so in change down there already. Save your money for the souvenirs across the street—you'll need it.

THE ELVIS PRESLEY AUTOMOBILE MUSEUM

The Automobile Museum is the newest and slickest attraction at Graceland. Before it was built, fans on the Graceland tour could see Elvis's cars in the carport. But now—for a separate admission, of course—you can eyeball 20 vehicles and car-related Elvisiana in an air-conditioned fifties setting.

The highlight is Gladys's famous 1955 pink Fleetwood Cadillac. Elvis bought it for Mom with his first record money, even though she didn't drive; it was a

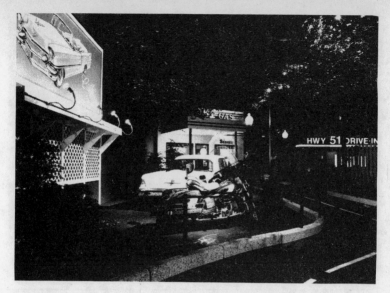

A stroll down Memory Lane in the unique and exciting settings of the car museum. Hey, I didn't write this—it's in the press kit.

symbol. A home movie of Gladys, Vernon, and the Caddy plays next to the vehicle.

The best of the rest:

- The stunt-double Cobra from *Spinout*
- Elvis's 1971 Stutz Blackhawk—the first ever delivered—and the 1973 Blackhawk seen in the last photo of Elvis ever taken
- Elvis toys: a golf cart, go-cart, dune buggy, snowmobile, pedal car, and three-wheeled Supertrike
- Elvis's Harleys and cycle gear

The Hwy 51 Drive-in, in the center of the museum, presents an entertaining 10-minute compilation of automotive Elvis movie clips produced by Steve Binder, who also produced the 1968 Singer Company TV special, "Elvis." To watch, you sit in car seats and listen through actual drive-in speakers.

Elvis's Stutz at the car museum. Note Gladys's pink Caddy in the background.

THE *LISA MARIE*

The *Lisa Marie* is a Convair 880 jet, manufactured in December 1958 by General Dynamics in San Diego. It was part of the Delta Airlines fleet until it was purchased by Elvis in April 1975 and converted into the *Lisa Marie*. He bought the plane for $250,000 and spent more than $846,000 refurbishing it, including painting the TCB logo

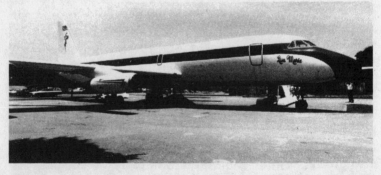

The *Lisa Marie* appears ready to take off—except that the wings would probably fall off.

on the tail. The *Lisa Marie* became part of Air Elvis in November 1975: its capacity was 28, its nickname was Hound Dog One, and it could go 3,000 miles without refueling. For the year 1976 it cost $404,000 to operate.

Significant events on the *Lisa Marie*:

- Elvis used the plane to fly to Denver for peanut-butter-and-banana sandwiches.
- Lisa Marie celebrated her ninth birthday on her namesake.
- Elvis was about to take off on the plane for Portland, Maine, the day he died.
- After Elvis died the CIA used the plane to transport a deposed Central American dictator to a friendly South American country.

After Elvis's death, the *Lisa Marie* was bought by an Evangelist who hoped to make money selling tours of the plane across the USA and Europe. He didn't, and the plane was then sold to International Automotive, Inc. It ended up in Fort Lauderdale before returning to Memphis International Airport February 6, 1984; its wings were clipped and it was towed through the streets to Graceland accompanied by marching bands.

The self-guided tour of the *Lisa Marie* attraction begins at a mock boarding area, where you watch a short film before passing through the Elvis-fan detector—the alarm goes off. Awwwright!

A path takes you first to Elvis's Jet Star plane, known as Hound Dog Two. You can't go inside; many visitors skip this. (The Jet Star is easily the most pointless attraction at Graceland.) On to the *Lisa Marie*. Inside, you'll see a sink coated with 24K gold flecks; even the seat-belt buckles are gold-plated. The conference room has a weird, fuzzy, Linda Thompsonesque centerpiece. The bed has a queen-size seatbelt strapped across its width. Video monitors tell you about the part of the plane you're in. It's opulent all right, but you don't get a strong sense of Elvis like you do inside Graceland.

THE TOUR BUS

Elvis bought this bus in 1959 and had George Barris convert it to his specifications. The floor and engine were lead-lined for soundproofing. Elvis liked to do the driving. You see a sample of the "stash of cash" that was discovered hidden in the bus when the rear door was installed for tours; the bills are kind of charred and singed. Check out those fuzzy pillows on Elvis's bed! The bus, on loan to Graceland from current owner Jim Sturm, is valued at $350,000.

THE ELVIS UP-CLOSE MUSEUM

This "rare glimpse of the 'personal' Elvis" is really just a less-exciting version of the museums run by Jimmy Velvet and Mike Moon. It's one small room, everything's distant and behind glass, and the line moves slowly, but there's lots of neat stuff, taken from Graceland's forbidden upstairs: Elvis's office, wardrobe room, and bedroom, Lisa Marie's nursery, and the attic.

Some advantages over other museums: a pamphlet describes each item, and there are no re-creations or defensive "proofs" of authenticity.

Highlights:

- Some of Elvis's wild furnishings, like the gaudy red chairs from the Linda Thompson era and a big, fuzzy bed with a big, fuzzy canopy
- His remote control box and gold-plated telephone
- His ¾" videotapes, including *The Return of the Pink Panther* (Elvis was a Peter Sellers fan), Monty Python, and the Ali-Norton fight (There's also an autograph from Ali: "Elvis, you are the greatest.")

- His paychecks from Precision Tool and M. B. Parker Co., Inc.
- Lisa Marie's crib
- A letter inviting Elvis to perform for the Queen of England
- Grandpa Jessie Presley's war-ration book

Graceland officials are thinking about dumping Elvis Up-Close; the high-tech Automobile Museum seems to be the wave of the future.

IF I CAN DREAM

A bonus for those who buy the combination ticket to all Graceland attractions is the "let's run some Elvis clips together and call it a movie" film *If I Can Dream*. But if you're going the à la carte route, skip it. It's too hard to get in a movie-watching mode with so much *real* stuff to see.

$ $ $ $ $

GRACELAND TICKET INFO

Prices are subject to change, if you know what I mean. Checks, money orders, Visa, MasterCard, and AmEx are accepted.

	Adults	Seniors	Kids 4-12
Combo (everything)	$15.95	$14.35	$10.95
Graceland only	7.95	7.20	4.75
Automobile Museum only	4.50	4.05	2.50
Planes only	4.25	3.80	2.75
Elvis Up-Close	1.75	1.75	1.75
Bus only	1.00	1.00	1.00
If I Can Dream	1.50	1.50	1.50

For information and tickets, call: (800) 238-2000, or

(901) 332-3322 in Tennessee. Or write to P.O. Box 16508, 3734 Elvis Presley Boulevard, Memphis, Tennessee 38116-0508. June–August, 8:00 A.M.–7:00 or 8:00 P.M.; September–April, 9:00 A.M.–6:00 P.M.; May, 8:00 A.M.–6:00 P.M. Closed Thanksgiving, Christmas, New Year's Day, and Tuesdays from November–February.

$ $ $ $ $

THE HEARTBREAK HOTEL RESTAURANT

This diner used to be in downtown Memphis, where it was called "The Kings' Heartbreak Hotel Restaurant."

The best neon in Memphis.

You can still see this on the sign, but it's not an ungrammatical reference to Elvis: the owners were a Mr. and Mrs. King. When the Kings divorced, Graceland bought the fixtures and relocated the restaurant here, mainly because of its snazzy neon sign.

The pink Studebaker out front has no Elvis connection whatsoever. That hasn't stopped it from becoming one of the most photographed cars in the world. Many assume it's Gladys's pink Caddy, but it's not—that one's inside the Automobile Museum.

The restaurant itself is, alas, about as forlorn as its namesake. Its main virtues are that you can get some of the dishes found in Vester Presley's *The Presley Family Cookbook* and you can be with a whole lot of fellow Elvis fans while you eat. There are lots of fast-food outlets nearby, but if you don't want to repark the car, your only other option at Graceland is the Echo Papa Snack Shop, which fries up burgers. (Echo Papa is control-tower talk for EP, and you know what that stands for.)

THE GIFT SHOPS

There's no gift-shop deficiency at Graceland, but in the last few years offbeat, unique Elvis souvenirs have become harder to find than true facts in an Albert Goldman book. Graceland has done such a tenacious job protecting Elvis's name, likeness, and image and ensuring good taste that there's not a whole lot of delight in any of the seven shops here. Your options are:

The 880 Echo Papa Gift Shop
EP's LPs (soon to be EP's CDs?)
The 50% Off Gift Shop
The Gotta Get to Memphis Gift Shop
The Graceland Gift Shop

The Graceland Photo Shop

The "Relive the Magic" Museum and Gift Shop

You never know who you'll find here, however: the day I visited, Elvis's Uncle Vester was pressing the flesh and autographing copies of his books, *A Presley Speaks* and *The Presley Family Cookbook*.

GRACELAND GIFTS: THE ELVIS PRESLEY CATALOG

Since Graceland has standardized the Elvis souvenir industry, the items have become less of an impulse buy and more the stuff of mail-order catalogs. You can get a copy of the catalog or place an order by calling (800) 238-2000 [(901) 332-3322 in Tennessee]. Highlights are:

Glittery gold satin jacket with Vegas Elvis on the
    back: $54.95

TCB necklace: $7.95

Elvis coffee mug with a handle in the shape of a
    musical note: $4.99

Elvis "history mug," with brief résumé printed on
    side: $4.99

High-quality black satin jacket with Elvis and pink
    Caddy on back: $165

ELVIS COLOGNE

History's first Elvis scent debuted on January 8, 1991. Priscilla, who often complained about Elvis's erratic toilet habits, had a fragrance already. Here's a description of hers, Moments: "Opens with a chypre floral blending of cassis, orange flower, ylang-ylang and jonquille. As the top notes fade, they give way to a seductive and romantic floral body achieved through a combination of jasmine, rose muguet and tuberose. Finally, anchoring the scent with a warm and alluring base are the essences of sandalwood, patchouli and moss, mingled with musk and vanilla for a lasting effect."

Well, the Elvis scentmeisters weren't about to let that sit. Here's their description of Elvis, the Cologne: "A fresh, contemporary, masculine blend of woods, herbs, and amber. The sparkling introduction bursts with crisp notes of cypress, armoise, sage, and lavender. The heartnote pulsates with extracts of precious woods: patchouli, vetiver, sandalwood, and fir balsam. Warm amber and musk blended with smoldering encens and oakmoss create the haunting, sensual residual of this unique creation."

The bottle's shape is inspired by Graceland's architecture. It's all housed in a blue box, because that was Elvis's favorite color. The promotional slogan is an understatement: "America has had 41 presidents . . . but only one King." For info call (800) 523-0907.

INTERNATIONAL TRIBUTE WEEK

Graceland is a supernatural experience any time of year, but if you want to be there when the whole place (*all* of Memphis, in fact) is pulsating with Elvosity, you have to go in mid-August, during International Tribute Week.

There are several ways to get advance information. Certainly, any fan club would provide details, and you can meet fellow members in Memphis. Or you can call Graceland and ask to be put on a mailing list for the calendar of events, which is published in late spring. Or you can subscribe to *Graceland Express*, a quarterly newsletter published by the folks at Graceland that costs $12 a year (P.O. Box 16508, Memphis, Tennessee 38186-0508). Some events, especially the concert (see Events), sell out quickly, so get tickets in advance. Most events that charge admission donate the proceeds to charity.

The annual Candelight Service, held every August 15, is the highlight, allowing you entrance to the grounds during hours it is usually closed. Elvis Presley Boulevard is technically off limits to auto traffic during the night of the service, but all you have to do is tell the first officer who approaches your car that you're going to pay your respects to the King, and you'll be waved through. Parking is free—just drive on in to the lot across from Graceland.

Be prepared to wait in line to get in. No matter what time you arrive—the official starting time for the service is listed in the Tribute Week schedule—you'll probably be standing outside of the gates for at least an hour. This is the time to chat with friends and fellow fans, sing Elvis tunes, take pics of King lookalikes, etc. If you forgot to bring a candle, you can buy one here, but don't light it—you'll get your fire from the eternal flame at the entrance to Graceland.

As you walk through the gates, you'll want to compose yourself and file "silently and reverently" up the drive, as the service program suggests. This is *not* the time to chat or sing. This is the time to think about Elvis and what he meant to you and to the world. If hot candle wax drips onto your hand, just you keep it to yourself.

The procession to Meditation Garden is slow and quiet. The grounds are lit with spotlights of blue and green, and the sounds of Elvis's wistful ballads waft through the muggy air via well-placed speakers. If you're the emotional type, keep that hanky handy. Many fans also bring small mementos to leave at Elvis's grave: a single red rose, perhaps (very popular), or maybe a small teddy bear.

There's no hurry here—you can stay as long as the

service continues, which is usually until around three o'clock. The Graceland gates remain open until everyone files past the graves. Most restaurants on the boulevard stay open real late that night, so when you've filed out of Graceland you can go sit for a spell, have a peanut-butter-and-banana sandwich, and ponder the experience.

EVENTS

EVENTS SPONSORED BY GRACELAND

Nostalgia Concert

A performance by artists who worked with or admire Elvis. This is one of the hot tickets. The 1990 lineup included the Judds, the Jordanaires, and Bruno Hernandez, a four-year-old Elvis impersonator.

Sock Hop

Live band plus disc jockey. Another one to buy in advance.

Elvis Trivia Contest

Daily elimination heats during the week. No charge for spectators or contestants. At Graceland Plaza.

Elvis Art Exhibit and Contest

Elvis-themed art—some for sale, some not—is displayed all week in the Graceland visitor center. No charge, but you must contact Graceland in advance if you want to participate.

Elvis Video Nights

Concert footage, films, home movies, and rare footage are shown at Graceland Plaza for free. Specific program available during EITW.

Meditation Garden

All year, the garden is open free to the public for 90 minutes before the first tour of the day. During EITW it's open 6:00 A.M.–7:30 A.M., with additional hours after closing, 8:30 P.M.–10:00 P.M.

5K Run

There's a small entry fee, but you get a T-shirt and vie for prizes. Register in advance or on the morning of the race.

Elvis Presley Memorial Karate Tournament

Top choppers from around the world compete.

"Elvis Legacy in Light" Laser Light Show

All week, at the Pink Palace Museum. Two matinees daily, evening shows on weekends. For advance tickets call (901) 454-5609 or write Pink Palace Museum Planetarium, 3050 Central Avenue, Memphis, Tennessee 38111.

ELVIS WORLD Breakfasts

In the Elvis Room of Shoney's, 3641 Elvis Presley Blvd. For reservations write to *ELVIS WORLD* magazine, Box 16792, Memphis, TN 38186.

Fan Club Get-Togethers

Many are open to anybody. Consult schedule.

Special Tours

Tours are arranged to such meccas as the Kang Rhee Karate Institute, the Elvis Presley Memorial Trauma Center, Tupelo, the Walls ranch, Humes High, and Sun Studio.

THE BIRTHDAY CELEBRATION

The annual Birthday Celebration, which fills three days around January 8, is becoming a bigger deal every year, though it's still nothing like Tribute Week. On the night of the eighth there's a charity banquet, themed to various aspects of Elvis's life. The 1991 banquet, for example, commemorated the 30th anniversary of Elvis's USS *Arizona* fundraiser.

Other events include a sock hop, free-video night, expanded visiting hours at the Meditation Garden, and a proclamation of Elvis Presley Day. Contact Graceland in December for specific info.

TRAVEL TIPS

When's the best time to visit? Well, you'll have lots of elbow room in the winter, but even at the peak of summer, when the wait for the Graceland tour without reservations can be up to three hours, you can use that time to tour the *Lisa Marie*, the Automobile Museum, and Elvis Up-Close, see *If I Can Dream*, buy souvenirs, eat at one of the restaurants. . . . There's plenty to fill the waiting time.

A reservation assures you of a specific tour, however, if you're on a tight schedule. Just call Graceland and give your credit card number or mail a cashier's check or money order. (The latter require at least two weeks for clearance. Personal checks require six-weeks' advance.)

You might consider visiting between Thanksgiving and the birthday celebration: Elvis loved Christmas, and the impressive Graceland Christmas display has become a ritual.

Memphis's weather is pretty mild in the winter, but it rains a lot. During the summer Memphis is hot—very, very, hot.

5
Nashville

Elvis was really not a Nashville kind of guy. The hip-shakin', rhythm & blues mentality of Memphis suited him far better than the country conformism of Nashville. But Nashville is Music City, and sometimes Muhammad has to go to the mountain.

After bombing at the Grand Old Opry, young Elvis repaired to his grass roots and forged a career so instantaneously successful that when he returned just over a year later to begin recording at the RCA studio, he was the hottest act in show biz.

Elvis never hung out in Nashville except when recording; the Colonel lived here, however, in suburban Madison. In November 1955, at the Andrew Jackson Hotel, Elvis was signed to RCA Records. His New York City–based music-publishing company, Hill and Range, had offices here. (Hill and Range has since been bought by Unichappell Music in Los Angeles.) Elvis's personal physician in the 1970s, Dr. Nick, graduated in 1959 from Nashville's Vanderbilt University Medical School. And in March 1961, Governor Buford Ellington stood up in the

General Assembly of the State Legislature in Nashville and declared Elvis an honorary colonel—just like his manager.

THE KING IN COUNTRY MUSIC LAND

Elvis performed just once on the Grand Ole Opry, in September 1954. He sang "That's All Right (Mama)" and "Blue Moon of Kentucky"; according to most accounts, including Elvis's, the Opry's booking agent, Jim Denny, told him to go back to driving a truck. Nonetheless, the brochure for the **Ryman Auditorium** tour brags of his appearance here. It's a significant spot for all music lovers, and it's got a gift shop, so I recommend a tour despite the way they treated Elvis.

The Ryman is downtown on Fifth Avenue North, just north of Broadway. Open 8:30 A.M.–4:30 P.M. every day except Thanksgiving and Christmas. Admission is $2; kids under 12, $1. (615) 254-1445.

The Opry relocated in 1974. If you want to see the modern-day version, you can get info from the **Grand Ole Opry** Ticket Office, 2808 Opryland Drive, Nashville, Tennessee 37214, or call (615) 889-3060. The Opry is located off the Briley Parkway.

The voters for the **Country Music Hall of Fame** have so far also snubbed Elvis, but that doesn't prevent their museum from displaying the coolest Elvis car in creation.

George Barris did such a great job customizing this Fleetwood Cadillac that Elvis couldn't possibly drive it anywhere without creating a rubbernecking nightmare. The concept is *gold*. Inside is a solid-gold TV set, and gold records are embedded in the interior roof. There's also an electric shoe polisher and a 45 rpm record player. These aren't cunningly designed on-the-go versions of household appliances like you might expect; no, they're actual standard models plunked down inside a car.

In the 1960s, this gold Caddy toured the world in Elvis's stead.

Since Elvis didn't tour in the sixties, RCA, which paid for the customizing, sent the Cadillac all over the world in his stead. The car was donated to the museum before Elvis died; at that time it was the only Elvis item officially on display anywhere in the world. Since the uniqueness of this car was its interior, the museum had the Caddy roof made removable: it lifts up and away at the push of a button.

The museum, besides being an excellent tribute to country music, has many exhibits of interest to Elvis fans. Two primo items are the guitar Elvis used in the 1954 Sun sessions and his gold lamé stage jacket from 1970–71. Also on display are Elvis the Horseman's saddle, bridle, and breast collar—possibly solidifying his "country" credentials?

There's also memorabilia from Carl Perkins and Johnny Cash, Elvis's Sun buddies. But after the Elvis Caddy, the most popular exhibit here is probably the Bandit Car, which Burt Reynolds drove in *Smokey and the Bandit II*. The Elvis connection? The film costarred

Jerry Reed, who wrote two great Elvis songs: "Guitar Man" and "U.S. Male."

The Country Music Hall of Fame and Museum is at 4 Music Square East. June–August, 8:00 A.M.–8:00 P.M.; September–May, 9:00 A.M.–5:00 P.M. daily. For info, call (615) 256-1639.

The Country Music Foundation also runs tours of **RCA's Studio B**, where, from 1958 to 1971, Elvis recorded such songs as "Are You Lonesome Tonight?," "Crying in the Chapel," "(You're the) Devil in Disguise," "Good Luck Charm," "It's Now or Never," "Little Sister," "She's Not You," and "U.S. Male." His producers during this period were Roy Acuff and Felton Jarvis.

You first have to go to the Country Music Hall of Fame to get admitted here; it's free with Hall of Fame admission. An informative booklet about Studio B, which closed in 1977, is sold at the Hall of Fame gift shop.

In the hallway outside Studio B you'll see a display of Felton Jarvis's gold records for *Elvis Sings the Wonderful World of Christmas*, *Elvis Country*, and *How Great Thou*

The Elvis display at the Country Music Hall of Fame.

RCA's Studio B, where Elvis cut his Nashville tracks.

Art. (Altogether, Elvis recorded about 20 gold records here.) You'll also see the original soundboard that was used for these hits.

On the studio tour, you get a demonstration of multi-track recording and see the Steinway piano on which Elvis would play while singing gospel tunes to get warmed up for a recording session.

Studio B is at Roy Acuff Place and Music Square West, formerly Hawkins Street at 17th Avenue. Before November 1957, however, it was located at 1525 McGavock Street, in a space rented from a bunch of Methodists. At this site, Elvis did his first recording for RCA, including "Heartbreak Hotel" and "I Got a Woman." Now it's a television studio for Jim Owens Productions, from which The Nashville Network's "Crook and Chase Nashville Music Show" is broadcast.

Jimmy Velvet's **Elvis Museum & Gift Shop** is no longer graced by the presence of Dee Presley, Elvis's attractive stepmother, who would sign autographs, pose for photos, and talk to visitors, but it's still a must for Elvis fans. Velvet, the world's foremost Elvisiana collector, stocks this and another museum in Kissimmee, Florida. He also has two portable exhibits touring the U.S.A. and another tooling through Europe.

The collection, which is overwhelming, spans Elvis's career. Early artifacts include the original 1817 family Bible, some of Dr. William Hunt's tools (he delivered Elvis, but got stiffed on his fee), Elvis's withholding statement from 1952 (he earned $109), and a 1953 Humes High yearbook with an inscription from the King ("Best wishes to a swell guy").

Elvis's Hollywood days are represented by his Beverly Hills Mercedes (a cardboard Elvis peeps out through the sunroof), a gun used in *Viva Las Vegas*, the bed and headboard from his Hollywood home, and a champagne glass from his wedding and Graceland reception.

Elvis's final years yielded the most excessive and varied objects. One reason is that Elvis's continual weight shifts led him to buy and discard clothing at a feverish pace. The museum displays a TV set shot out by Elvis, his last jumpsuit (powder blue), a photo of Elvis with Nixon that sat on Elvis's desk for years, a Star of David watch with a cross that lights up every 20 seconds (designed by Elvis and Marty Lacker), and a bulletproof vest. Velvet also salvaged many items—including the soundboard and the engineer's seat—from the defunct American Sound Studios in Memphis, where Elvis recorded his great 1969 albums.

1520 Demonbreun Street, on Music Row. Open daily 8:00 A.M.–10:00 P.M. (615) 256-8311.

Here's a major boo-hoo: Elvis A-Rama, an 85-foot-long, 10-foot-high mural depicting the life of Elvis, accompanied by a dramatic computerized sound-and-light show introduced by Dick Clark, was closed in the late eighties. Sonny James had proclaimed it "a spectacular work of art." One hopes some rich art lover with a big room is preserving it for our grandchildren.

Dee Presley, Elvis's stepmom, lures travelers into the Elvis museum in Nashville.

Is Elvis "country" or not? Consult your local wax-meister:

The **Country Music Wax Museum and Shopping Mall** has a figure of the King, along with Roy Acuff and others who were important to Elvis. It's at 118 16th Avenue South, in the Country Music Mall, on Music Row. Open June–August, 9:00 A.M.–9:00 P.M.; September–May, 9:00 A.M.–6:00 P.M. Admission: $4 adults, $1.75 kids.

Another wax Elvis can be found at the **Music Valley Wax Museum of the Stars**. Out front is the Sidewalk of Stars, the country-music equivalent of Mann's Chinese Theater in Hollywood. It's just off Briley Parkway, west exit 17A, at 2515 McGavock Pike. Open June–August, 8:00 A.M.–9:00 P.M.; September–May, 9:00 A.M.–5:30 P.M. Admission: $3.50 adults, $1.50 kids.

The **Car Collectors Hall of Fame** has an Eldorado that Elvis bought in Denver in 1976 at 2:00 A.M., after rousing the dealer out of bed. You'll also find a copy of the original script for *Jailhouse Rock*, as well as the Hot Rod Hearse from "The Munsters." 1534 Demonbreun Street, on Music Row. (615) 255-6804.

BITS AND PIECES

The **Television News Archives** of the Vanderbilt University Library has copies of all network news coverage of Elvis since 1955. West End Avenue, north off I-440. For info and appointment, call (615) 322-2927.

Elvis stayed at the **Sheraton South Motor Inn**, 737 Harding Place, while recording in late 1976, before he flew back to Memphis to be with his girlfriend, Ginger Alden. Res.: (615) 834-5000.

Finally, only one musician played on recordings of both Elvis and Buddy Holly—saxophonist **Boots** Randolph. He has a nightclub in Printers' Alley, between Union and Church Streets. Res. and info: (615) 256-5500.

PARKERLAND

Eddy Arnold, Colonel Parker's first big show-biz client, gave the Colonel and his wife a place he owned in Madison just to get them out of his own home; it became the **Parkers' residence** for years, until they moved to Palm Springs. And it's a striking residence indeed. Like Graceland, it's both unmistakable *and* smack in the center of a congested commercial strip. The perimeter is marked by an ugly chain-link fence, and the entire front "yard" is paved. Stone lions flank the driveway gate. A "see the homes of the stars" tour bus stops here. Elvis would often camp here with the Colonel while in town recording.

1221 Gallatin Road, just south of Due West Boulevard.

Madison was also the 1827 birthplace of Dunnan Presley, Jr., Elvis's great-great-grandfather. Dunnan liked

Colonel Parker lived many years at this home outside Nashville. Note the lovely lawn and gardens—not!

to do things in twos: he was a bigamist who twice deserted the army. He left his family in Tennessee to marry Martha Jane Wesson, Elvis's great-great-grandmother, in Itawamba County, Mississippi.

DAY TRIPS

The **Willie Nelson Showcase** in Hendersonville's Music Village includes a display on J. D. Sumner and Elvis. Music Village is a museum complex adjacent to Conway Twitty's mind-boggling self-monument, Twitty City. It's on Music Village Boulevard. (615) 882-1800.

At the nearby **House of Cash**, you can view the actual bed that Johnny Cash and June Carter slept in during the first few years of their marriage. And that's not all! Among other things, Johnny's stocked the place with Sun memorabilia and a one-piece-at-a-time Cadillac that was built from Caddy parts dating from 1949–1973.

700 Johnny Cash Parkway. Open April–November, Monday–Saturday, 9:00 A.M.–4:30 P.M. Closed Sundays and holidays. $6 adults, $1 kids 6–12. (615) 824-5110.

ROAD TRIPS

Bristol: In 1976 the owner of the **Bristol Holiday Inn** donated bedsheets Elvis once slept in to an auction for the local Episcopal Church Day School. Elvis had stayed here, and presumably slept here, while performing nearby in March of that year. The aluminum foil that Elvis had placed over the windows to block out light was donated to the Bristol Humane Society, cut into strips, and sold for a dollar per square inch. Flowers from the room were given to crippled children. At the end of his stay, a buxom woman ran up to Elvis as he was leaving the motel, tore off her shirt, and offered herself to the King. Elvis smiled and strode on.

Exit 74B off I-81. Res.: (615) 968-1101.

As long as you're in town, you might as well check out the country's largest guitar-shaped building. It's the **Grand Guitar Museum**, 535 New Kingsport Highway. (615) 968-1719.

Gatlinburg: The **World of Illusions** makes this promise: "See a spectacular illusion: Elvis sings again." Don't believe it. A dim light comes on to illuminate a cheap "holographic" projection of Elvis's head. What a burn. Highway 441. Open daily, 10:00 A.M.–10:00 P.M. (615) 436-9701.

Equally misleading is the **Guinness World Records Exhibition Center**, which features *two* Elvis photos in its brochure and advertises him at the entrance. All they have are some photos and a dinky TCB touring jacket. Highway 441. (615) 436-9100.

Stars Over Gatlinburg has a wax seventies Elvis on display in a belting-out-a-song pose. Highway 441, at the Reagan Terrace Mall.

Luttrell: Chet Atkins, who played guitar on some of Elvis's Nashville tracks, was born here.

Maynardville: Roy Acuff, Elvis's first Nashville producer, hails from this small town.

Pigeon Forge: In late 1990, 33-year-old Kentuckian **Eddie Miles** began performing "**A Salute to Elvis**" at the Memories Theatre. His show, which reflects the early seventies Vegas Elvis, but also often salutes the black-leather, 1968 Christmas Special King, has received kudos from hardcore fans, justifying the slogan, "You loved Elvis . . . You'll love Eddie." Check out these comparisons:

- Name: 5 letters starting with "E"
- Birthdate: 8 (January versus March)
- Shoe size: 12

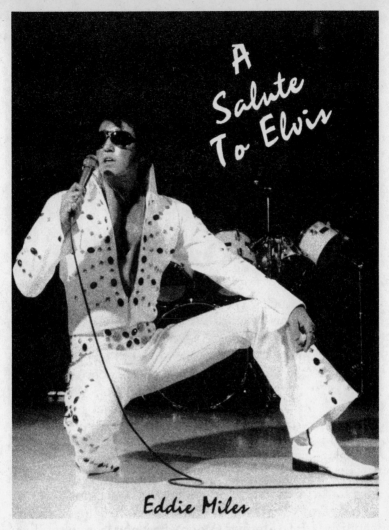

A Salute To Elvis

Eddie Miles

Eddie Miles: not an impersonation, but a salute.

Eddie makes Pigeon Forge, and the Memories Theatre, his base six months a year, spring through autumn. The rest of the time he's out touring. After the show, stay for autographs and meet Eddie. You can also buy T-shirts, scarves, cassettes, videos, and buttons.

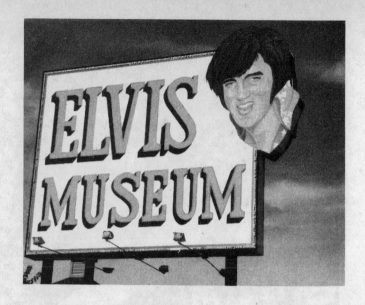

The Memories Theatre is on the Parkway (Highway 441), at the north end of town. Children under 12 get in free with adults. Info: (615) 428-7852.

The **Smoky Mountain Car Museum** has Elvis's 1971 Mercedes 280 SEL; a Hank Williams, Jr., car customized with 547 silver dollars; James Bond's Aston-Martin from *Goldfinger* and *Thunderball*; Buford Pusser's 1968 Toronado patrol car; and Billy Carter's service truck.

Highway 441. Open July–Labor Day, 9:00 A.M.–8:00 P.M., shorter hours spring and fall.

Elvis collector Mike Moon is giving Jimmy Velvet a run for his money, with **Elvis Presley museums** here and in Niagara Falls, Ontario. Moon has accumulated memorabilia via J. D. Sumner (Moon's best connection to Elvis), as well as Guys like Charlie Hodge, Marty Lacker, and Sonny West. Moon says he did management and promotion work for Elvis in 1970.

The big-time Elvisiana on display is highlighted by the "$250,000" TCB ring that Elvis gave to Sumner, a backup singer. (The price is totally speculative—Sumner refuses to sell; it's here on loan.) Elvis's Hollywood bed-

The Smoky Mountain Car Museum has Elvis's 1971 Mercedes along with vehicles of James Bond and Billy Carter.

Elvis's Lincoln limo, at the Elvis Presley Museum in Pigeon Forge.

room set is here; look but don't sit. The car here was Elvis's last white Lincoln limo.

But it's the smaller items that make this place special; they truly afford a glimpse into the everyday Elvis. For example, learn how his generosity would cause him literally to give away the clothes off his back by seeing the suede coat that was bestowed on security guy John O'Grady when Elvis noticed an ink stain on it. Or the black fur coat that was given to Elvis by Charlie Hodge: Elvis later gave it back to Hodge, allegedly saying, "Since you liked this coat well enough to buy it for me, I'd like for you to have it back."

Elvis's "fun-loving practical joker" side is made manifest by an authentic pair of panties that Elvis put on Sumner's head after they were thrown onstage. There's also a pair of Elvis's leather gloves that has sand sewn into the knuckles to provide extra punch, his pump shot-

n is one of the last brushes that Charlie Hodge
n the last concert tour. There are three others.
    ...were used on the last tour. Two belong
                ...where - the third is still in the

Nasal Spray Applicator
    This pink nasal spray applicator was used by Elvis on the last tour also. It's purpose was to remedy emergency sinus attacks that Elvis often had.

Fate was smiling upon Mike Moon the day he found this nasal spray applicator for his museum in Pigeon Forge.

Get "inside Elvis" by studying his x-rays at the museum in Pigeon Forge.

gun, .38 special (with his actual bullets), and the DEA sweat suit he liked to wear.

Elvis's health-care products are here: his razor (Schick Flexamatic), massager, nasal spray applicator, hair dryer, and Brut cologne.

A couple of the odder displays here are a set of x-rays (on a light table) from Desert Hospital in Palm Springs, with diagnosis, and something called "Elvis's First Dollar," which he left on a collection plate at the Highland Assembly of God church in Meridian, Mississippi, and later signed. Moon paid $8,000 for it in 1982.

The gift shop offers standard Elvis purchases, but you can also pick up copies of his karate-school diploma and weekly grocery list (topping off the list: King Cotton bacon).

On the Parkway (Highway 441), one block south of Ogle's Water Park. Open daily, 9:00 A.M.–10:00 P.M. (615) 453-6499.

6
Hollywood

Since nobody before him had ever had a lasting career in rock & roll, Elvis resolved early on to become a movie star rather than a singer. From his 1960 army discharge until the end of the decade, Elvis made movies full-time. His only new records were feeble sound tracks, and eight years passed before he made another live appearance.

Elvis's routine in the 1960s was to shuttle between Graceland and Hollywood on his customized bus. Life on tour in the 1970s may have been tiring, but at least Elvis had the gratification of pleasing a live audience. Elvis felt no such pride in his work of the sixties; he constantly deprecated his films and sound tracks—though his very presence makes all of them a pleasure to endure.

Elvis, the highest-paid star of the era, rarely made the Hollywood scene—he would have been mobbed. But he did leave his mark around town, filming at different studios, recording sound track albums, and shopping.

WHERE ELVIS SLEPT

When Elvis was in Hollywood from 1956 to 1958 making four films, Colonel Parker booked him and the Guys into hotels. Not until his 1960 return from the army did Elvis and his rowdy entourage move into a rented house. Considering that Elvis made about three films per year from 1960 on—and that he was rich—it's surprising that he never bought a house here until his marriage, in 1967. Elvis and the Colonel also had houses in Palm Springs, where the Colonel dwells today.

Elvis stayed at the **Knickerbocker Hotel**, on Ivar Avenue, a few times during recording sessions and filming. He and the Guys took over the 11th floor. Elvis quartered his parents here on Gladys's only Hollywood visit, during filming of *Loving You.* (She and Vernon appear in the film as part of an audience. After Gladys died, Elvis refused ever to see the film—not that he would watch his movies anyway.) The Knickerbocker is now a senior-citizen's hall.

Elvis might have also stayed a few times at the **Roosevelt Hotel**, 7000 Hollywood Boulevard, which recently was remodeled to its former art deco splendor. If Elvis did stay here, he probably would have been put in the Celebrity Suite, which rents for $1,500 per night. Res.: (800) 950-ROOS; (213) 466-7000 in Los Angeles.

But the Beverly Wilshire is the one place where Elvis and crew would reside time and again, even though the stuffiness of the environment was hardly congenial to the heartiest partiers in Hollywood. (More recently, Julia Roberts offended propriety here in *Pretty Woman.*) It's now the **Regent Beverly Wilshire**, 9500 Wilshire Boulevard, at Rodeo Drive. Suites cost $500–$600 per night; the cheapest room is $255. Res.: (213) 275-5200.

In 1960 Elvis rented the first of four leased Holly-

The snooty hotel seen in *Pretty Woman* is where Elvis and the Guys partied in the fifties and early sixties.

wood homes, in Bel Air, at **565 Perugia Way**, adjacent to the Bel Air Country Club golf course. The home had previously been occupied by the Shah of Iran, as well as by Aly Kahn and his wife, Rita Hayworth. Elvis's neighbors included actress Greer Garson and Pat Boone.

The pseudo-Oriental house was built in a semicircle around a garden and waterfall; Elvis converted the garden to a rec room. There were parties here every night; the most common activity was watching Elvis watch TV. It was here that Elvis received the Beatles in August 1965. The house appeared in the *Elvis and Me* TV movie in 1988. But in 1990 this historic structure, modest by ostentatious-mogul standards, was demolished, and an enormous mansion was constructed in its place.

Elvis tried moving to a different Bel Air home in 1963; it was larger and had a bowling alley in the basement, but Elvis found it too big and creepy, so the gang soon returned to Perugia Way and stayed there till 1965.

The historic Elvis house on Perugia Way—where he met *the Beatles*, for gosh sakes—has been demolished to make way for some stupid megamansion.

The address that appears in several sources, **1059 Bellagio Road**, is impossible to find—just a warning.

In late 1965 Elvis found another rental in Stone Canyon, a modern house at **10550 Rocca Place**, near the Bel Air Hotel. He and Priscilla lived here during their first few months of marriage. Then it was a one-story California ranch; now it's a two-story English Tudor. A later owner added a tennis court, something Elvis never would have done.

Soon after the wedding, Elvis became a Hollywood homeowner for the first time, plunking down $400,000 for a faux chateau in Trousdale Estates, at **1174 Hillcrest Road**. *Ooh, la, la*—this is one Elvis-cile that looks today as it did back then; subsequent owners have even preserved the iron gate on which fans scrawled messages. The newlyweds' neighbors included fellow Memphis biggie Danny Thomas, who was, like Elvis, rumored to have "peculiar" dining preferences.

In May 1968, a few months after Lisa Marie was

The iron gate where fans would scrawl messages, at 1174 Hill-crest.

born, the family moved to a house at **144 Monovale Road**, in Holmby Hills, that had once been owned by actor Robert Montgomery. (His daughter, Elizabeth, was Samantha on "Bewitched.") When Elvis and Priscilla separated in the early seventies, Priscilla remained here and Elvis camped with the Guys at the Trousdale house. The Monovale house was sold to Telly Savalas in 1975. It looks today much as it did then, except that Kojak replaced the front lawn with a tennis court.

Elvis also built a house in Palm Springs, at **825 Chino Canyon Road**, with the backing of the Colonel, who had made his permanent base here. The Spanish-style, white-stucco ranch, surrounded by a fence, cost Elvis $85,000. He did some recording here in September 1973. The house was willed to Lisa Marie, but it was sold in 1979 to Frankie Valli for $385,000. It looks pretty much today as it did when Elvis was here.

Elvis also leased a 5,000-square-foot house on a Palm Springs estate, at **1350 Leadera Circle**, in 1967. He and Priscilla spent their wedding night here, flying from Vegas in Frank Sinatra's Lear jet, the *Christina*.

Colonel Parker and his wife have lived in Palm Springs for years at **1166 Vista Vespero Drive**. The address is listed in Elvis's personal phone book on display at the Pigeon Forge Elvis museum.

POST-ELVIS PRISCILLA

Priscilla began drifting away from Elvis in the Hollywood days. She attended Mike Stone's karate school in Westminster so she could "get to know him." They ended up living together in a cozy love nest in Belmont Shores; Elvis often considered sending assassins there to dispatch Stone.

In 1973 the divorce was made final in a Santa Monica courtroom. After gaining an increased settlement from Elvis, Priscilla moved to **1167 Summit Avenue**. The following year she opened Bis and Beau's, an instantly successful Beverly Hills boutique, at 9650 Santa Monica Boulevard. She sold her interest in 1976; at the site now is Giannino's, an Italian fast-food place. When Lisa Marie married fellow Scientologist Danny Keough, Priscilla bought them a house in the valley, in Tarzana.

SHOPPING

Elvis ordered his first giveaway TCB necklaces from Schwartz and Ableser Jewelers; they were designed by Lee Ableser. According to Ableser's son, the company was able to expand thanks primarily to Elvis's patronage. Nowadays, **Ableser's Fine Jewelry** sells TCBs to the public; their best customer is Elvisologist extraordinaire

Here's the mold used to make TCB jewelry
at Ableser's.

Jimmy Velvet. The cost fluctuates with the price of gold.
251 North Beverly Drive, Beverly Hills. (213) 274-3088.

George Barris, the Kustom Kar King, created the tour bus on view at Graceland and the gold Elvis Caddy at the Country Music Hall of Fame, in Nashville. On display in the **Barris Kustom Industries** showroom is a gold Elvis Dream Cadillac, with an EP hood ornament, gold-ukulele armrests, electronic baubles, guitar sun visors, fuzzy gold dice dangling from the rearview mirror—a rolling domain of gold plushness. 10811 Riverside Drive, North Hollywood. (213) 877-2352.

Nudie Cohn, of **Nudie's Rodeo Tailors**, fashioned several Elvis outfits through the years, including the gold lamé suit seen on the cover of the *50,000,000 Elvis Fans* album. There's a wall of portraits and rack of clippings pertaining to the country-music stars Nudie has attired; an oil painting of Nudie and Elvis—decked out in the hot,

The plush gold Elvis car at George Barris's showroom. Barris customized vehicles for the King.

Nudie's, home of outrageous celebrity rodeo fashions, is a country musician's wet dream.

Inside Nudie's Rodeo Tailors, a painting of Nudie Cohn with Elvis, decked out in the famous gold lamé suit.

heavy gold suit—is prominently featured. 5015 Lankershim Boulevard, North Hollywood. (213) 877-9505.

The Dennis Roberts Optical Boutique supplied the nearsighted Elvis with over 400 pairs of prescription TCB sunglasses. The store was at 9525 Brighton Way, in Beverly Hills. After Elvis died, Roberts went bankrupt and moved to Las Vegas; the site is now a Mark Cross store. Also gone is Kerr's Sporting Goods, the snooty shop in Beverly Hills where Elvis bought many expensive guns.

Elvis didn't seek only material gratification in Hollywood; he accoutered his spirit at the **Self-Realization Fellowship**, which was founded by Guru Yogananda. Elvis and Priscilla visited the branch at 3880 San Rafael Avenue, on Mt. Washington in the Hollywood hills [(213) 225-2471], but more often Elvis went to the visitor-friendly Pacific Palisades branch.

Elvis consulted Brother Adolph, an old monk, in Pacific Palisades. Here, the tourist can enjoy a gift shop, the Yogananda Museum, and the Lake Shrine, where a coffer

The Meditation Garden at Graceland was based on the Lake Shrine at the Self-Realization Fellowship.

contains some of Gandhi's ashes. The Meditation Garden at Graceland was obviously inspired by the Lake Shrine. 17190 Sunset Boulevard, three blocks from the ocean. Open Tuesday–Saturday, 9:00 A.M.–4:45 P.M.; Sunday, 12:30 P.M.–4:45 P.M. (213) 454-4114.

MR. HOLLYWOOD

Elvis had his first screen test, for producer Hal Wallis, at **Paramount Studios**, 5451 Marathon Street, in Hollywood; he was good enough to snag a three-picture deal. In 1956, while in town shooting his first movie, *Love Me Tender*, Elvis ambled over to **CBS Television City**, at Fairfax Avenue and Beverly Boulevard in Los Angeles, for his first appearance on "The Ed Sullivan Show." It earned the highest ratings in the history of the world to that date.

The **Conejo Movie Ranch**, near Thousand Oaks, was used as a location in 1960 for *Flaming Star*. *Roustabout* was also shot around Thousand Oaks, as well as in Hidden Hills, in March 1964.

The Hidden Lodge resort, which was in Idyllwild, just west of Palm Springs, was used for *Kid Galahad* exteriors in 1961. *Kissin' Cousins* was shot around Big Bear Lake in October 1963. Los Angeles locations for *Spinout* (1966) included Dodger Stadium and the Ascot Motor Car Racing Ground. *Live a Little, Love a Little* was shot in 1968 at the Los Angeles Music Center, in the offices of the *Hollywood Citizen-News*, along the Malibu coastline, and at Marineland of the Pacific.

Elvis's sensational Singer Christmas special was shot in the summer of 1968 at **NBC Studios**, 3000 West Alameda Avenue, Burbank. And the offices of Colonel Parker were in Culver City, home of MGM studios. His firm was called Elvis Exploitations.

Studio 56, formerly Radio Recorders, where Elvis cut his sound-tracks in the sixties.

AND HE CAN SING, TOO

Elvis did his first, most, and best L.A. recording at Radio Recorders, in Hollywood. His output here included: "All Shook Up," "Can't Help Falling in Love," "Hard Headed Woman," "King Creole," "Love Me Tender," "One Broken Heart for Sale," "Return to Sender," "Teddy Bear," "That's When Your Heartaches Begin," and "Treat Me Nice."

The place is still a recording studio, **Studio 56 Productions**. It's at 7000 Santa Monica Boulevard, and even though you can't see anything here, it's worth a visit. Why? Check out the sidewalk at the foot of the street sign on the corner—notice some **familiar graffiti** scratched into the cement? It says "Elvis '57"! It's impossible to verify, but. . . . Try not to steal it, fans.

At the now-defunct Hollywood RCA Studios, Elvis

recorded sound tracks and the songs "Always on My Mind," "Burning Love," and "Rags to Riches." At the MGM sound studio, in Culver City, he recorded some songs for *Speedway* (1967), *Live a Little, Love a Little* (1968), and others. In 1968 he recorded some tracks for *The Trouble with Girls* at United Recorders and the theme song for *Charro!* at Samuel Goldwyn Studios, both in Los Angeles. The following year he did tunes for *Change of Habit* in Universal City, at Decca Recording Studios.

SOUVENIR CORNER

Here's one for the Elvis fan who has everything. "Between Takes with Elvis" is a three-record set (no cassettes or CDs) of Elvis and friends talking between takes, both in concert and in the studio. This sumptuous collection includes "Elvis Speaks About the Hot Weather and Recalls Ripping Many of his Jump Suits Onstage" and "The Complete Water Pistol Fight." It's peddled by Jerry Osborne and Creative Radio Shows for an extortionate $39.95, plus $3.00 shipping. P.O. Box 11203, Burbank, California 91510.

Handsome, fit, and slightly cross-eyed wax Elvis at the Hollywood Wax Museum.

STILL REMEMBERED

More than any other entertainer, Elvis dominated both the record business and the movie business. For his **star on Hollywood Boulevard**, however, only one of the potential two standard icons—a phonograph record or a movie camera—would fit: it was decided to salute his musical achievements. Probably a good call. 6777 Hollywood Boulevard, east of Highland Avenue.

Just a few doors down from the star is the **Hollywood Wax Museum**. Inside you'll find an Elvis figure in a pink jumpsuit; the top is zipped down and his slim, hairy chest is exposed.

6767 Hollywood Boulevard, near Highland Avenue.

Open daily, 10:00 A.M.–midnight; Fridays & Saturdays 10:00 A.M.–2:00 A.M. (213) 462-8860.

Since 1988, the most musical birthday tribute to the King has taken place at L.A.'s **Palomino Club**, 6907 Lankershim Boulevard. The 1991 jam lasted four hours, with local talent playing "sixty songs learned in six hours." Not only did earnest rockabilly middleweights knock out a special Sun Sessions re-creation, but Woody Harrelson, the stupid bartender from "Cheers," performed his patented rendition of "Jailhouse Rock."

El Vez, a popular Hispanic Elvis impersonator, provides the East L.A. version of Hot Springs, Arkansas' Buford Presley—a parody act played primarily for laughs. El, backed by his quartet of lovely Elvettes, has been known to croon "You Ain't Nothin' but a Chihuahua."

The Scientology Celebrity Centre. "Visitors welcome"— not! And celebrities? Morgan Fairchild was nowhere in sight!

FROM ELVIS TO L. RON

If you ask, you will be told that the 1988 "public" wedding of Lisa Marie and Danny Keough and ensuing celebration took place on a cruise ship in the Caribbean, not at the **Church of Scientology Celebrity Centre**, in Los Angeles. No, you are informed, this is merely where the actual, private ceremony took place—not that it's any of your business, since you were not invited. Despite its encouraging name and friendly appearance, this place is neither chock full o' stars nor begging for public perusal. 5930 Franklin Avenue.

? ? ? ? ? ? ?
USING ELVIS TO PREDICT THE FUTURE

Elvis's L.A. hairdresser got him "into" spiritual matters in the sixties. Part of this was the study of numerology, which was used to determine a given course of action. In other words, Elvis would use his numbers to predict the future. And so can you!

The key numbers in Elvis's life were 8 and 2,001. Elvis was born 1/8/35. Since $1 + 8 + 3 + 5$ equals 17 and $1 + 7$ equals 8 (all numbers must be reduced to one digit), *Elvis was an 8*. Now, if you add up the month, day, and year that Elvis died (8/16/1977) you get 2,001. This becomes doubly eerie when you learn that Elvis rented office suite 2001 in the Commerce Bank Building at 2001 Union Avenue. Now, what song was played as an overture to Elvis's Vegas shows? That's right, "Theme from *2001: A Space Odyssey*"!

Clearly, these are blessed numerals, and you can use

them to help guide you in life. For example, let's say you're at the race track. The number eight horse in the eighth race is called "Gladys's Boy." Bingo! Or let's say you're

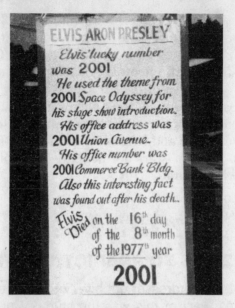

Elvis and the number 2001—an eerie affinity.

looking for an apartment. You see an ad for a place at 2001 Eighth Street, apartment 8EP. Pounce on it! Finally, you meet a very special someone, and learn that he or she was, like Elvis, born January 8, has a brother named Jesse, and works at the 2001 Disco. What to do? Forget it—who wants to date someone who works in a disco?

???????

7
Las Vegas

Vegas and Elvis were a perfect match: to both, nighttime is the right time. But Elvis's first Vegas gig in 1956 was disastrous; back then, he was considered shocking and rebellious—two adjectives they don't use on Vegas marquees. He returned in 1963 to film one of his most entertaining movies, *Viva Las Vegas*. In 1967 he slipped away to get married here in relative secrecy. But he became a veritable totem of Vegasosity in 1969 with his stunning comeback concerts at the new International Hotel. And he lives on, with many tangible evidences of the King's former rule.

One spot not on our tour is the residence of Elias Ghanem, the house doctor of the Hilton who tended to Elvis and provided him with drugs. Ghanem's upper-floor bedroom was designed as a retreat for Elvis. If you insist on exploring this aspect of Elvis's Vegas Years, you can visit **Landmark Drugs**, where Elvis would cop pills when in town. It's at 252 Convention Center Drive, in the Somerset Shopping Center.

NO FUN IN THE FIFTIES

Elvis made his first Vegas debut in April 1956 at the **New Frontier Hotel** (now simply the Frontier). He was billed as "The Atomic-Powered Singer," appearing in the Venus Room for $17,500 per week as the opener for Shecky Green, and was met with indifference. Thus spake *Variety*: "For the teenagers, he's a whiz; for the average Vegas spender, a fizz. His musical sound with the combo of three is uncouth, matching to a great extent the lyric content such as 'Long Tall Sally,' 'I Got a Woman,' 'Money Honey' and other such ditties."

Although the Atomic-Powered Singer bombed, Elvis dug Vegas, especially the nightlife, the showgirls, the glitz, the showgirls, and the showgirls. He came here for a brief vacation in November 1956, and was photographed backstage at the **Riviera** with Liberace. It's a famous novelty shot: Elvis held a candelabra, Lee strummed a guitar. Elvis got Lee's autograph for his mom. On a 1957 visit he held a summit with another Vegas legend; Elvis dated Tempest Storm, a Hall of Fame stripper.

The Frontier no longer has a Venus Room; in fact, the hotel has been completely remodeled. 3120 Las Vegas Boulevard South. Res.: (800) 634-6966.

VIVA LAS VEGAS

The King made a grand return to Vegas in July 1963, sweeping into this desert oh-waste-us to shoot *Viva Las Vegas* with Ann-Margret, who would become a local institution herself within a few years. He and Ann-Margret stage an energetic dance number in a ratty-looking gymnasium at the **University of Nevada, at Las Vegas** (4505 Maryland Parkway), which has since become a formidable through still NCAA-sanctioned basketball power. Locations at the **Tropicana** (3801 Las Vegas Boulevard South) include the Folies Bergere, where Elvis and his Continental rival search for Ann-Margret, and the skeet-shooting range, where A-M outguns the King. The swimming pool at the **Flamingo** (3555 Las Vegas Boulevard South) is where Elvis and Ann-Margret croon the knockout "The Lady Loves Me" duet.

During filming, Elvis stayed in the Presidential Suite—his entourage took most of the top floor—of the **Sahara Hotel**, 2535 Las Vegas Boulevard South. Res.: (800) 634-6666. The Presidential Suite is reserved for VIPs and high rollers and must be booked through management.

WEDDING BELLS

On May 1, 1967, Elvis and Priscilla obtained a marriage license at 3:30 in the morning in the **Clark County Clerk's office**, 200 South Third Street. The office is still open 'round the clock on weekends, 8:00 A.M. till midnight on weekdays. They wed that morning in the second-floor suite of Milton Prell, owner of the **Aladdin hotel**, and held a press reception afterward.

The Aladdin is now co-owned by Wayne Newton, the guy who more than anyone else took Elvis's place as Mr. Vegas—yes, it's hard to believe, but keep in mind that the closest thing to Elvis in modern movies is the reptilian Prince.

3667 Las Vegas Boulevard South. The second-floor Prell Suite has been broken up into separate rooms. The good news is, you can book the actual room where Elvis was married. The bad news is, nobody seems to know

"If Elvis ever remarried, he would have done it here."

exactly which room that would be. Res.: (800) 634-3424.

Yes, it might be fun to get married at the Aladdin, but consider the **Graceland Wedding Chapel**. Here, for only $150, you can have an authentic Elvis impersonator witness your wedding. He will perform for a good solid half-hour, and you can record it on video.

Johnny Lawson is the primary Elvis torch-bearer here. "We've never had anyone disappointed with the Elvis impersonator," says a spokesperson. "He's going to make the big time. . . . He sounds so much like Elvis, you could close your eyes and swear it was him." Nick Guerrero is the backup Elvis. Both also appear locally. About two couples are wed the Elvis Way per week—they're almost always big fans.

Elvis's marriage license is on display; if you buy the basic $45 wedding, you get a free copy. Jon Bon Jovi, a big Elvis fan, was married at Graceland Chapel in May 1989. There's a sign out front about this, also about "Falcon Crest"'s Lorenzo Lamas getting wed here. "If Elvis ever remarried," the spokesperson asserts, "he would have done it here."

619 Las Vegas Boulevard South. Info and res., call (702) 382-0091.

COMEBACK CITY

When the Colonel booked Elvis as the second act to play the new Las Vegas International (the first was Barbra Streisand), Elvis knew he would need to put on a *big* show, not the scruffy stuff he did here back in 1956 with Scotty and Bill, when they were merely in the process of inventing rock & roll as we know it. He had seen his pal Tom Jones wow large, middle-aged audiences in Hawaii and here at the Flamingo, and wisely took a lesson in how to please a Vegas crowd.

When Elvis hit town in July 1969 to play the 2,600-seat Showroom Internationale—he was booked for four

You can have an authentic Elvis impersonator witness your wedding at Graceland Chapel. "On the Strip"!

weeks at $125,000 a week—he hadn't performed live in eight years, and success was far from guaranteed. Needless to say, though, it was one of the hottest engagements in entertainment history. Elvis generally did two shows a night, at 8:00 P.M. and midnight.

In 1971 the International became the **Las Vegas Hilton**. The Colonel, who had gambling disease and was given many special perks by Hilton management—including a year-round three-room suite—committed his boy for 13 subsequent engagements faster than you can say "conflict of interest." Elvis's first live-performance film, *Elvis—That's the Way It Is*, was shot here in August 1970. The Hilton awarded Elvis a $10,000 gold-and-diamond belt for bringing in unprecedented business.

Elvis lived in the 30th floor Imperial Suite, now known as the **Elvis Presley Suite**. (Only headline entertainers can stay here, but the room can be booked for special events.) Priscilla told Elvis good-bye in this room. George Klein, one of the principal Guys, was married here—Elvis served as his best man. And it was here in this sanctuary that Elvis shot out a TV during a Robert Goulet song. That'll teach 'im!

In September 1978, Colonel Parker held a 10-day fan convention. Always Elvis, here. Priscilla and Vernon dedicated a 400-pound bronze statue of Elvis by Carlo Romanelli; it was placed near the entrance to the main showroom. The statue, in a "reaching out to touch the audience" pose, is sequestered behind a plexiglass cylinder. You can see scratch marks, probably from fake fingernails, on the outside part of the case closest to Elvis's finger.

There's also a bronzed Elvis guitar in a case nearby, as well as a Vegas jumpsuit and a plaque with a semicoherent inscription from Barron Hilton; it reads, in part: "None of us really, totally, know how great a performer he was. . . ." Huh?

The Colonel was booted from his suite, Room 446–447, soon after Elvis died. It's now reserved for VIPs and high rollers, and must be booked through management.

The Las Vegas Hilton is at 3000 Paradise Road, behind the Riviera. Be sure not to confuse this with the Flamingo Hilton on Las Vegas Boulevard. Res.: (800) 732-7117.

EVEN MORE ELVIS

The **Vegas World** hotel has some of the best fifties-era neon in town, and boasts a nightly performance by Elvis impersonator E. P. King (not his real name). You can catch E.P. handing out scarves and teddy bears in the Galaxy Theater every night (except Thursday) at 6:00 P.M. Res. and info: (702) 383-5264. 2000 Las Vegas Boulevard South.

The **Imperial Palace** also presents an Elvis impersonator as part of its "Legends in Concert" show. The other featured performers are Marilyn Monroe, Buddy Holly, Liberace (a little too chubby), Michael Jackson, and Neil Diamond facsimiles. Shows Monday through Saturday. Info and res.: (800) 634-6441.

The 200-car collection at the **Imperial Palace Auto Museum** includes an early-seventies Elvis Cadillac. It's on the fifth floor of the parking garage at the Imperial Palace Hotel, 3535 Las Vegas Boulevard South. The museum's open daily, 9:30 A.M.–11:30 P.M. Admission: $6.95. (702) 731-3311.

The "World of Las Vegas" section of the **Guinness World of Records Museum** has on display one dinky album that says "Elvis's Golden Records." A plaque explains: "Most golden disks ever awarded to an individual." This is a shameful underrepresentation of the man who *was* Vegas for many years; Wayne Newton practically gets a whole wing here. If you want to go complain, it's at 2780 Las Vegas Boulevard South. Open 9:00 A.M.–midnight. Admission: $4.95. (702) 792-3766.

8
Elvis Around the World

Colonel Parker was a foreigner without proper papers, and that's why Elvis played every little corner of the U.S.A. but almost never left the country to perform. This accounts, partly, for why the Elvis mystique is so strong overseas. Elvis sang in Canada only three times, all in 1957. He was offered astounding sums to appear in England (including 2 million pounds to play Wembley Stadium), Australia, and other countries, but the cowering Colonel rejected all overseas propositions.

AUSTRALIA

Melbourne: In November 1977 the Elvis Presley Fan Club of Victoria (see Elvis Fan Clubs) erected a sleek, impressive **memorial** to the King in Melbourne General Cemetery.

Elvis rules "down under": the classy memorial in Melbourne, Australia.

CANADA

Niagara Falls, Ontario: The 5,000-square-foot **Elvis Presley Museum** was opened in 1979 by collector Mike Moon, who also runs an Elvis museum in Pigeon Forge, Tennessee. The collection includes a 1967 Coupe de Ville known as "Elvis and Priscilla's honeymoon Cadillac" and a 1964 Lincoln convertible. There's also "Elvis's favorite casual suit," an ornate living-room lamp from Graceland, and x-rays of Elvis's hand.

Moon tells us he owns a bottle of champagne presented to Elvis by the Denver restaurant that used to make his peanut-butter-and-banana sandwiches as well as an eight-millimeter home movie of a Biloxi fishing trip with Elvis, Vernon, and Gladys. He might put these on display in the near future.

In Maple Leaf Village mall, off Clifton Hill. (416) 357-0008.

ENGLAND

London: Madame Tussaud's, the world's most famous wax museum, has a notoriously unflattering Elvis statue that fans just don't like. Also in London: Marvin Benefield, an Elvis "soundalike" whose stage name is Vince Everett (Elvis's character in *Jailhouse Rock*), opened an **Elvis Presley Museum** here in 1983. There's **Rising Sun Pub**, unofficially known as Presley's Pub, at 46 Tottenham Court, plays all-Elvis music on Sundays. And Chinese Elvis impersonator Paul Chan holds forth at his two **Graceland Palace** Chinese restaurants.

Wales: Peter Singh, a turban-wearing Pakistani Elvis impersonator, performs at various venues in Swansea.

FRANCE

Paris: Elvis jumped onstage and sang at the famous **Lido** nightclub while in the army in 1959. He stayed at the **Prince de Galles Hotel**.

The house at Goethestrasse 14 where Elvis lived while in the army. No plaque, no memorial—nichts. Das ist schade.

GERMANY

Bad Nauheim: Upon their arrival in West Germany in October 1958, Elvis, Vernon, and Minnie Mae briefly checked into the **Park Hotel** while looking for a house to rent, but other guests complained about all the hubbub from fans and in less than a month it was "suggested" that they move on. Before the hotel was demolished in 1990, it had on display the original guest register with Elvis's signature. Just like with the Quedlinburg treasures, however, someone has absconded with that book.

From there they moved to the **Hotel Grünewald**, at Terassenstrasse 10. They took the entire top floor *plus* a large bedroom one floor below just to store bags of fan mail.

They soon found a five-bedroom white stucco house at **Goethestrasse 14** and paid the equivalent of $800 a month to live there for the remainder of the 15 months that Elvis was overseas in the army. The house is now owned by a doctor.

There are no plaques to commemorate the most exciting thing that ever happened to this town, because civic leaders (or, as they say in German, *die dummkopfe Bürgermeister*) just don't seem to care. In October 1988, a life-size Elvis statue, funded by German and English fan clubs, was dedicated in the port of Bremerhaven to commemorate the 30th anniversary of Elvis's arrival there on the USS *General Randall*. It was brought to town for a fan-club meeting but was returned to England soon after.

Friedberg: Elvis was stationed at **Ray Barracks**, which maintains an Elvis Room crammed with memorabilia. The dining facility has been named after him, and the barbershop where the King routinely had his locks shorn to army specs has become a shrine, with clumps of Elvis hair and The Comb on display to this day.

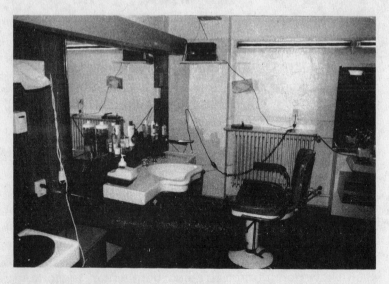

Locks of Elvis's hair and his comb are on display at this army barbershop in Germany.

Ja, ja, ja! Private Elvis
having fun at the
Moulin Rouge night
club, Munich.

Captain Joseph Beaulieu was stationed here at Wiesbaden Air Force Base in late 1959. His daughter Priscilla met Elvis soon after their arrival.

Munich: Elvis took some R and R in Munich at the now-shuttered Moulin Rouge nightclub, Bayerstrasse 141. He partook of the local fun and frauleins, but the revelry was broken up by a fight involving one of Elvis's army buddies. Faster than you can say, "Hey, here come the M.P.s," Elvis was outta there.

SWEDEN

Munkedale: This small town, a veritable hamlet, has an **Elvis Presley Museum**, dedicated in 1984. It's on the E-6, two hours north of Goteborg, on the route to Oslo, Norway. The curator is Bruno Tillander. Currently, the museum's artifacts are on tour, so call ahead if you want to visit.

Elvis Fan Clubs

The following fan clubs are just about the best in the
world.

Blue Hawaiians for Elvis Fan Club
Box 69834
Los Angeles, CA 90069
Contact: Sue Wiegert

Burning Love Fan Club
1904 Williamsburg Drive
Streamwood, IL 60107
Contact: Bill DeNight

Elvis Fans from Hoosierland
37 S. Lynhurst Drive
Indianapolis, IN 46241
Contact: Sharon Ott

Elvis, Heart of Gold Fan Club
P.O. Box 126
Kahoka, MO 63445
Contact: Jeanne Brewer

Elvis Memorial Fan Club of Hawaii
Box 15120
Honolulu, HI 96815
Contact: Charlie Ross

Elvis Presley Fan Club
P.O. Box 82
Elsternwick, Victoria 3185
Australia
Contact: Wayne Hawthorne

Elvis Presley
Gesellschaft, e. V.
Postfach 19 29
W-4770 Soest
Germany
Contact: Peter Kranzler

Elvis Worldwide Memorial Fan Club
3081 Sunrise
Memphis, TN 38127
Contact: Will "Bardahl" McDaniel

Eternally Elvis TCB, Inc.
2251 N.W. 93rd Avenue
Pembroke Pines, FL 33024
Contact: June Poalillo

It's Elvis Time
Postbus 27015
3003 LA, Rotterdam
Holland
Contact: Peter Haan

Let's Be Friends with Elvis
Thaddaeus-Robl-Strasse 9a
8000 Munich 45
Germany
Contact: Sabina and Michael Witzel

Oklahoma Fans for Elvis
421 W. Sixth Street
Bristow, OK 74010
Contact: Bill and Judy Wilson

Oklahoma Fans for Elvis
714 Catherine
Duncan, OK 73533
Contact: Keith Mitchell

Presley-ites Fan Club
6010 18th Street
Zephyrhills, FL 33540
Contact: Kathy Ferguson

Tidskriften Elvis
Box 4506
S-175 04 Jarfalla
Sweden
Contact: Ake Flodin

We Remember Elvis Fan Club
1215 Tennessee Avenue
Pittsburgh, PA 15216-2511
Contact: Priscilla Parker

Welcome to Our Elvis World
5648 Arnhem Road
Baltimore, MD 21206
Contact: Pat Carr

The Wonder of You
277 Magothy Blvd.
Pasadena, MD 21122
Contact: Dorothy Kimes

States that have approved
Elvis Day, January 8

Official "Elvis Day" Map

Bibliography

American Graphic Systems. *I Am Elvis*. New York: Pocket Books, 1991. This alphabetical collection of Elvis Impersonator bios isn't exactly gripping, but what can you expect from an author named American Graphic Systems?

Cotten, Lee. *All Shook Up: Elvis Day-By-Day, 1954–1977*. Ann Arbor, MI: Pierian Press, 1985. It's hard to believe this exists, but if you can't trace Elvis's every move, whose can you trace? Many minor errors, especially on things like spelling, but what a job of research!

Edwards, Michael. *Priscilla, Elvis and Me*. New York: St. Martin's, 1988. Only mentioned as a warning not to buy. Albert Goldman's is by far the most mean-spirited Elvis book, but what Edwards has written is not only superslimy but it also has nothing whatsoever to do with the King.

Geller, Larry, and Joel Spector, with Patricia Romanowski. *If I Can Dream*. New York: Simon & Schuster, 1989. Geller was Elvis's "spiritual advisor," and you just know that his long, loud voodoo sessions with the King must have pissed off the Colonel and the Guys to no end. For that reason, you gotta like him. As with most of the "insider" books, you get the impression that the author was the only person in whom Elvis could truly confide.

Goldman, Albert. *Elvis*. New York: McGraw-Hill, 1981. This "best-smeller" is the main reason why so many Americans have a screwed-up impression of Elvis.

Greenwood, Earl, and Kathleen Tracy. *The Boy Who Would Be King*. New York: Dutton, 1990. Recollections of Elvis's second cousin. Good stuff about the hazy early days of the King, with stories about his shiftless ancestors. Once again, the author seems to be the only one in whom Elvis could truly confide. So how come you never hear about Earl in any of the *other* books?

Hammontree, Patsy Guy. *Elvis Presley: A Bio-Bibliography*. Westport, CT: Greenwood Press, 1985. Looks pointy-headed but is actually a well-measured examination of Elvis and his mystique—with most of the facts sorted and straightened out.

Latham, Caroline, and Jeannie Sakol. *E Is for Elvis*. New York: NAL, 1990. Some nice tidbits, but it can't touch *Elvis: His Life from A to Z*.

Presley, Priscilla. *Elvis and Me*. New York: Putnam, 1985. Big seller, but short on revelation and insight. Ever since reading the Michael Edwards book, my opinion of Priscilla has shot way down. How could she stand that goon? Nobody's *that* good in bed.

Stern, Jane and Michael. *Elvis World.* New York: Knopf, 1987. The most meticulously produced Elvis book of them all. Great photos, fun text.

Torgoff, Martin. *The Complete Elvis.* New York: Delilah, 1982. Lots of good random info and insights: a cornucopia of Elvosity.

Vellenga, Dirk, with Mick Farren. *Elvis and the Colonel.* New York: Delacorte Press, 1988. New research on the Colonel's early days, but poisoned by being totally unobjective—they hate the Colonel—not that he doesn't deserve it.

Worth, Fred L., and Steve D. Tamerius. *Elvis: His Life from A to Z.* Chicago: Contemporary Books, 1988. The most awesome assembly of Elvis factoids in print.

Yancey, Becky, and Cliff Linedecker. *My Life with Elvis.* New York: St. Martin's, 1977. Pleasant read by Elvis's former secretary, with lots of stories and a modicum of unsupported opinion mongering.

All photos are by the author except the following, which are courtesy of:

Index

at Circle G Ranch, 102–3
wedding dress of, 110
wedding of, 161
Presley, Vernon (father), 40,
48–49, 60, 109
Presley, Vester (uncle), 119–20
Priscilla, Elvis and Me (book), 13,
176
Promised Land, 83
Prowse, Juliet, 12

Racquetball, 111
Radio Recorders, 152–53
"Rags to Riches," 154
*Raised on Rock/For Ol' Times
Sake*, 83
Randolph, Boots, 133
RCA Records, 129
Reed, Jerry, 129
"Return to Sender," 153
Rhee, Kang, 91–93
Roustabout, 152

Scientology, Church of, 156–57
Screen test, first, 152
Self-Realization Fellowship,
151–52
"She's Not You," 25, 129
Sholes, Steve, 9
Shooting Room (Graceland), 109
Sinatra, Frank, 147
Singh, Peter, 168
Songfellows, 2
South Carolina, 37
South Dakota, 37–38
Speedway, 31, 154
Spinout, 110, 113
Starlight Wranglers, 82
Stay Away Joe, 4
Stone, Mike, 16, 147
Studio B (RCA Records), 129–31
Sullivan, Ed (TV show), 31, 152
Sun Records, 75–80, 135
Sweden, 171

"Teddy Bear," 153
Tennessee, 69–104, 126–41
fan club, 173

Texas, 38–43
"That's All Right (Mama)," 44, 77,
85, 127
"That's When Your Heartaches
Begin," 76, 153
This is Elvis, 24
Thompson, Linda, 46, 92, 107
"Tiger Man," 4
Tour bus, 116
"Treat Me Nice," 25, 153
Tribble, Iladean, 3
Tribute Week, 121–24
Trophy Building (Graceland),
109–10
Trouble with Girls, The, 154
"Turn Around, Look at Me," 5

Up-Close Museum (Graceland),
116–17
"U.S. Male," 129
Utah, 43

Vanderbilt University (Television
News Archives), 133
Velvet, Jimmy, 83, 116, 131–32
Vermont, 43
Virginia, 44–46
Viva Las Vegas, 5, 131, 159–60

Wales, 168
Washington (D.C.), 9–10
Washington (state), 46–47
Wax museums, 133, 136, *155*
Wedding (Elvis and Priscilla), 161
"Welcome Home, Elvis" (TV
special), 12
West, Bobby, 72, 74
West Virginia, 47
Westmoreland, Kathy, 55
White House, 9
Whitman, Slim, 82
Wild in the Country, 7
Williams, Hank, 3
Wilson, Regis, 83
Wisconsin, 47

Yancey, Becky, 56